I0620505

FISHING
FOR
MEN

Register This New Book

Benefits of Registering*

- ✓ FREE **replacements** of lost or damaged books

- ✓ FREE **audiobook** – *Pilgrim's Progress,* audiobook edition

- ✓ FREE information about new titles and other **freebies**

FISHING
FOR
MEN

Fishing Tips for Soul-Winners

J. WILBUR CHAPMAN

We enjoy hearing from our readers. Please contact us at www.anekopress.com/questions-comments with any questions, comments, or suggestions.

Fishing for Men

© 2024 by Aneko Press

All rights reserved. First edition 1904.

Revisions copyright 2024.

Please do not reproduce, store in a retrieval system, or transmit in any form or by any means – electronic, mechanical, photocopying, recording, or otherwise, without written permission from the publisher. Please contact us via www.AnekoPress.com for reprint and translation permissions.

Unless otherwise indicated, scripture quotations are taken from the New American Standard Bible® (NASB), copyright © 1960, 1962, 1963, 1968, 1971, 1972, 1973, 1975, 1977, 1995, 2020 by The Lockman Foundation. Used by permission. www.Lockman.org.

Scripture quotations marked "KJV" are from The Authorized (King James) Version. Rights in the Authorized Version in the United Kingdom are vested in the Crown. Reproduced by permission of the Crown's patentee, Cambridge University Press.

Cover Designer: J. Martin

Cover graphic: bazzier/Shutterstock

Editors: M. Tracy, R. Clark

Aneko Press

www.anekopress.com

Aneko Press, Life Sentence Publishing, and our logos are trademarks of

Life Sentence Publishing, Inc.
203 E. Birch Street
P.O. Box 652
Abbotsford, WI 54405

RELIGION / Christian Ministry / Evangelism

Paperback ISBN: 979-8-88936-419-1

eBook ISBN: 979-8-88936-420-7

10 9 8 7 6 5 4 3 2 1

Available where books are sold

Contents

Ch. 1: The Art of Fishing.. 1

Ch. 2: A Fascinating Work.. 13

Ch. 3: An Easy Work 25

Ch. 4: Personal Evangelism for Men...................................... 35

Ch. 5: How Some Men Have Been Won to Christ............ 45

Ch. 6: A Word with the Head of the House....................... 55

Ch. 7: A Never-Failing Principle.. 65

Ch. 8: A Startling Statement 79

Ch. 9: A Message to Men on the Grace of God................. 93

Ch. 10: A Church for Men 105

Ch. 11: Dr. Munhall's Message 123

Ch. 12: The White Life.. 135

Ch. 13: A Fatal Mistake 155

Ch. 14: Life or Death 175

J. Wilbur Chapman – A Brief Biography 189

To My Father
A Christian Gentleman, an Ideal Father
and a Priest in his Household

CHAPTER ONE

THE ART OF FISHING

Concerning the art of fishing, Dr. Henry Van Dyke, a successful fisherman, distinguished author, and great preacher, said,

The appeal of fishing for all ages, from the cradle to the grave, lies in its uncertainty. It is an affair of luck. No amount of preparation in the matter of rods and lines and hooks and lures and nets and baskets can change its essential character. No excellence of skill in casting the fly or adjusting the tempting bait upon the hook can make the result secure. You may reduce the chances, but you cannot eliminate them. There are a thousand points at which fortune may intervene. The state of the weather, the height of the water, the appetite of the fish, and the presence or absence of other fishermen can determine your success. When you go fishing, you just take your chances. You offer yourself as a candidate for anything that may be biting; you try your luck.

There are certain days that are favorites among fishers, who regard them as favorable for the sport. I know a man who believes that the fish always rise better on Sunday than on any other day in the week. He complains bitterly of this supposed fact because his religious principles will not allow him to take advantage of it. He confesses that he has sometimes thought seriously of joining the Seventh-Day Adventists.

But in fact, all these superstitions about fortunate days are idle and presumptuous. If there were such days in the calendar, a kind and firm God would never permit us to discover them. It would rob life of one of its principal attractions and make fishing altogether too easy to be interesting.[1]

While all this is true of fishing, it is not true concerning the art of fishing for men. When Jesus called His disciples, He said, *"Follow Me, and I will make you fishers of men"* (Matthew 4:19).

He makes them fishers as to their office, by His call, which is twofold – outward and inward – by setting them apart to the office of the ministry. It is our business to know whether we have been set apart for this work or not. He makes them successful fishers.

"You should consider it a great honor to be a catcher of souls!"

That is, He makes them catch men to Himself by the power of His Spirit accompanying the Word they preach.

Thomas Boston once said, "What an honorable thing it is to be fishers of men! You should consider it

---

1   Henry Van Dyke, *Fisherman's Luck* (New York: C. Scribner's Sons, 1899), 3.

a great honor to be a catcher of souls!" *We are God's fellow workers,* says the apostle Paul (1 Corinthians 3:9). If God has so honored you, oh you who are aware of this calling, then bless His holy name who called such a poor soul as you to be a coworker with Him. God has sent you to do good to those who were caught before. *Bless the LORD, O my soul* (Psalm 103:1). *Who am I, O Lord GOD, and what is my house, that You have brought me this far?* (2 Samuel 7:18).

Just to prove that it is possible for us to be sure of success, Jesus gives us the vision of His own gracious ministry and then sends out into the work men like Matthew, a tax collector, and of the opposite extreme a man like Peter, who was a profane fisherman. Both of them became equally successful in the art of fishing for men, so that one can readily see that it is not a question of natural gifts but rather a question of absolute yielding to Him who stands ready to equip us with power and skill for this most wonderful work.

One of the most fascinating fishing pictures in the New Testament is found in John 21. The scene is on the shores of the Sea of Galilee, where Jesus loved to be, and which was also an attractive place to His disciples.

After Jesus had been crucified and the disciples were like sheep without a shepherd, they were gathered one evening on the shores of the sea, watching the fishermen put out to their night's work. There is a peculiar fascination about fishing. If you have ever been skilled in this work, nothing can ever discourage you from it. And Peter was a real fisherman. With eyes flashing and face flushed, he turned to his fellow disciples to say, *"I am going fishing"* (John 21:3). His spirit stirred them, and they replied, *"We will also come with you"* (John 21:3). It was a poor night's work for them, for that night they caught nothing. Then there is given to us one of those beautiful gems of Scripture in which the Bible abounds – John 21:4-6. *But when the day was now breaking, Jesus stood on the beach; yet the disciples did not know that it was Jesus. So Jesus said to them, "Children, you do not have any fish, do you?" They answered Him, "No." And He said to them, "Cast the net on the right-hand side of the boat and you will find a catch." So they cast, and then they were not able to haul it in because of the great number of fish.*

It is well worth our while to notice the difference between the end of verse 3 and the end of verse 6. In the first we read: *They caught nothing.* In the second, it says, *Then they were not able to haul it in because of the great number of fish.* How can you account for the remarkable change in results? For you have the same sea, the same nets, and the same fishermen. To my mind, it is an easy problem to solve, and herein lies the secret of successful fishing for men. The first time they toiled in their own strength, the second time in the strength of their risen Lord. The first time they simply exercised their own ingenuity and fisherman's skill; the second time they perfectly obeyed the commands of Jesus who stood upon the shore saying, *"Cast the net on the right-hand side of the boat and you will find."*

During a recent visit to my home in Philadelphia, Reverend F. B. Meyer told me of his work with discharged prisoners. He was doing what he could to help them by means of a woodyard that was equipped with a splendid saw set on a strong frame and run by the discharged prisoners themselves. I was interested in this, because I had a desire to do the same thing for some men in Philadelphia, and the financial results were practically the same. At the close of each week, there was a deficit of funds. The woodyard scheme was unprofitable financially. Then Mr. Meyer said, "Someone suggested, 'Why don't you put a steam engine in your woodyard?'"

Following his suggestions, I set a little upright engine in operation. In the first week, the results were entirely different. Instead of losing money, I found I had actually made a profit. Then Mr. Meyer, this distinguished teacher and preacher, said, "I can imagine myself talking to the saw, saying, 'Old saw, what is it that has made such a difference in you? Up to this time, I have always lost money by you and now I see a significant change.' And if the old saw could speak," said my friend, "I do not doubt it would say, 'Well, master, you see, prior to this time I have been powered by men, but this week I have been propelled by the power of steam.'" And that was the secret of the successful week.

I do not doubt that many of us have failed in our fishing for men because we have worked simply in the power of the flesh. When the power of the risen Christ is behind us, success is very sure.

There are different ways of working. I know of one man who has given up everything – friends and home and comforts of every sort – that he may personally labor on behalf of the lost, and he has won dozens of men to Christ. Some men may feel, however, that they have little strength or talent to do the personal work for Christ.

I was told the other day of a wealthy man in St. Louis, who listened to a discussion of personal evangelism, and who, when it was over, came to his pastor to say, "See here, I cannot do this work myself; first, because I am too busy, and second, because I am sure I have no talent for it; but if you will find someone whom you know and ask him to devote his whole time to winning souls, I will assume his financial support for at least six months." This man did what he could for Christ by supporting others gifted in the work.

A certain Baptist minister who had worked fourteen years in a certain church never had a communion service in which he did not have the joy of welcoming many people into the church and to Christ. Men were amazed with his success. They studied his methods to find the secret of his power, all to no avail. When his pastorate came to an end and he was saying good-bye to those who could not in person say farewell to him, he came to an old bedridden saint who said to him, "Pastor, I have never heard you preach, but in all the time that you have been the pastor of our church, I have prayed for you without ceasing. Whenever I could not sleep, I prayed. And Saturday nights especially, I asked God for a great blessing to rest upon you on Sunday." The secret was out. This aged Christian man had all the time been winning souls, although he could not leave his room and rarely left his bed.

Praying for the Lord's ministers is another way

of doing this work for Christ, but whether we work, or pay, or pray, it must all be done in the strength of the risen Christ who has promised not only to make us fishers of men, but also to equip us with power to do the work. And when we work under His direction and leave it all with Him, what may have seemed to be insignificant in our sight becomes mighty in His, for when our weakness is coupled with His strength, no difficulty is too great to overcome. It is literally true that *[we] can do all things through [Christ] who strengthens [us]* (Philippians 4:13).

The story is told of an artist who fashioned a statue of an angel from marble and then sent invitations to his artist friends to look at his work and critique it. They were all loud in their praises. Michelangelo was there, too, and the artist, desiring to hear Michelangelo's comments

Whether our work is great or small, it amounts to nothing until the Master touches it.

without being seen, hid himself from view and with a fast-pounding heart heard the great artist say as he examined the work critically, "It lacks one thing." The poor artist was nearly brokenhearted when he heard what seemed to be unfavorable criticism made by the master. After days of suffering, he visited Michelangelo to hear from his own lips what was lacking in his work, and he heard the artist say, "It lacks only life to make it perfect. If it had life, it would move its wings and take its place among the angels in the skies and would be as perfect almost as God Himself could make it."

Whether our work is great or small, it amounts to

nothing until the Master touches it, and with that touch, it is absolutely sure of being crowned with success.

In the *New York Observer,* Arthur Howard Hall emphasized this thought from the standpoint of a poet:

> Upon the canvas long the artist wrought,
> With brush and pallet through each weary day.
> "Alas!" he sighed, "I but my faults display";
> And sinking on the floor with saddened thought,
>
> Soon fell asleep. The evening sunbeams caught
> Perfection's lights and shades in rich array,
> Because the Master's feet had passed that way—
> His skill had done what pity had besought.
>
> E'en so the Master who has gone above,
> Beholding how our work is crude and bare,
> In His own hands the tools doth often take,
> And by the strong transforming touch of love,
> For our surprise and honor doth prepare,
> Perfection's lines of beauty, ere we wake.

That distinguished preacher and soul winner, Reverend J. H. Jowett, of Birmingham, England, recently said in a sermon, "George Eliot was once listening to the complaints of some fisherman friends as they were describing their fruitless day's work. Looking into their empty baskets, she said, 'You should study the *subjectivity* of trout more closely.'" That is a very suggestive word, and significant for the fishers of men. We must study the fish so we may find out what will win them for the

Lord. All fish cannot be caught by the same bait. We must study the individual prejudices and habits and tastes. We must discover what will catch this man and that man and address ourselves accordingly.

I was once passing through a little village in the Lake District, and there was a card in the shop window that gave me more than a passing thought. On the card were a number of artificial flies with this engaging headline: "Flies with which to catch fish in this locality." The shopkeeper had nothing to say about the requirements of another region. He had studied the characteristics of the fish in his own neighborhood, and he had discovered what bait provided the best allurement.

We preachers must do this in our own localities. It was the practice of the apostle Paul: *To the Jews I became as a Jew, so that I might win Jews* (1 Corinthians 9:20). He became *all things to all men, so that [he might] by all means save some* (1 Corinthians 9:22). He baited his hook according to the fish he wanted to catch. I don't think we should fish with the same hook for Lydia and the Philippian jailer. It may be that we will discover that a sermon will never be effective. We may find out that a letter will do infinitely better work. Or it may be that a direct conversation is the appropriate approach. Or, again, it may be that an indirect conversation, apparently indirect and aimless, but quietly dropping one delicate hint, may win a soul for Christ. Study the fish!

Learn from other fishermen! Other men will never make us fishers, but they will make us better fishers. If we have the rudimentary gift, their experience may help to enrich it. Let us turn to the expert fishermen and see if their ways and methods can give us helpful advice. John Wesley was a great fisher; can we learn anything from him? Dr. Alexander Whyte has told us how he has made a patient and laborious study of John Wesley's journals for the purpose of classifying all the texts upon which the great preacher built his gospel message. Is that not a wonderful example for anyone who wishes to become skillful in this great ministry? What did Wesley preach about? And how did he fit his message to the changing circumstances of his varying spheres?

The Salvation Army in its early years had a great body of expert fishers. They lacked many things, but they caught fish. How did they do it? Many of their ways seemed strange to us, but what was it in their ministry that enabled them to win multitudes for the Lord? What was the secret of Finney and Moody? And what is it about Torrey that constrained the people to become disciples of Christ? Let us set about this investigation like men who wish to do great business for the Lord. Let us eagerly pick up any hints that these highly endowed and experienced men may be able to give us.

It has been said, "It is important to catch a trout early in your ministry. It gives someone more heart. It seems to help someone continue his business. Otherwise, you are apt to fall into unproductive reverie." I know no word more closely applicable to the work of the ministry. If we do not catch men, we are in great danger of losing even the desire to catch them. Our purposed activity is in peril of becoming a dream. Let me counsel my fellow preachers in the lay ministry to make up their minds to catch one soul, to go about it day and night until the soul is won. And when they have gained one man for Christ, I have then no fear as to what their resultant mood will be. The joy of catching a soul is unspeakable! When we have gotten one soul, we become possessed by the passion for souls. Get one and you will want a crowd!

And let me say this further word. Keep a list of the names of the souls you win for the King, and if on any day you are downcast, and the lightness and buoyancy goes out of your spirit, bring out that list and read it over, and let the contemplation of those saved lives make your heart sing and inspire you to fresh and more strenuous work. It is a good thing to have lists of the Lord's mercies by which to drive away the clouds in a day of apparent adversity. Let your labor be directed to the immediate catching of men for the Lord.

The joy of catching a soul is unspeakable!

And now I will close this meditation by offering a suggestion that I obtained from an advertisement in a fisherman's paper some time ago. "Now is the time for your old favorite rods to be overhauled and treated with a steel tonic that will not fail to work wonders in the way of renewing their strength." And following this advertisement came this confirming testimonial: "I am glad to acknowledge that a very whippy gig-whip of a rod has been converted into a powerful weapon." My hearers will immediately perceive the spiritual significance of the words. There are times when we need the "steel tonic" in order that our poor efforts may be

11

converted into powerful weapons. And, blessed be God, we have the promise of this redemptive work in the very names in which the Holy Spirit is revealed to us. He is called the Renewer, the Reviver, the Restorer of souls, and by His baptism the poorest, weakest agent can be turned into a powerful weapon. *Those who wait for the LORD will gain new strength* (Isaiah 40:31). Let us turn to our Lord this very night and seek that renewal in the strength of which we will turn to our work with multiplied possibility, and with perfect assurance of success.

CHAPTER TWO

A FASCINATING WORK

There is no joy that can be compared with that which rightfully belongs to a true servant of Christ. If men were seeking an experience of joy just from a selfish motive, I would advise an immediate entrance upon some form of Christian work.

Beyond every other experience known to man is the satisfaction that God has given to the one who really preaches the gospel, in no uncertain way, making no apology for his message, and believing it to be the very word of God and the power of God that is able to save to the uttermost. It is a joy to win anyone to Christ, for when we win the lost, we set joy throbbing in three places.

First. In the sinner's heart. There is nothing like that thrill that comes to the one who yesterday was in the darkness of sin, and today is in the clear light of the knowledge of God.

Second. In the worker's heart. It is actually beyond the power of human language to describe the joy that comes to the worker's heart. There must be great satisfaction in painting a masterpiece and making the canvas alive with the features of Jesus Christ, but it is not to be compared with the joy that comes to one in the possession of the knowledge that he has been used of God to bring to those who are lost and ruined by the power of sin the ineradicable likeness of Jesus Christ.

Third. In the heart of God. There is a text of Scripture that we frequently quote as follows: *There is joy in the presence of the angels of God over one sinner who repents* (Luke 15:10). And where is this joy most felt, but in the very heart of God himself? Is it not thrilling to know that we may have a share in a work that fills the heart of the Infinite God with joy?

The message must be personal... and practical.

While the general work of the minister has so much to be desired, I can truthfully say that there is no part of it so thoroughly fascinating as untiring service in the interests of men. But there are certain things that must be remembered if we are to move these special hearers. The message must be personal. Men enjoy being told where they are wrong if the one who is speaking tells them of their errors in the spirit of Jesus Christ. The message must be practical. The idea that some ministers have that the men of the world enjoy scientific and philosophical discussions is nonsense. When men come to the house of God, they come as a rule not to hear the things they have been thinking about all week, not to have discussed a proposition in which they may outrank in knowledge the speaker, but to hear that which has in it the very presence and power of God and breathes of the atmosphere of heaven. The message must be exceedingly plain. Men never admire a person without conviction in anything, and least of all do they admire him in the pulpit. In no uncertain way should the representative of Jesus Christ speak concerning the sinfulness of sin.

I was preaching not long ago in Chicago, when the following came to me from one of the men of the city: "I wish I might say something that would encourage you in your good work, and may I not write something that will express the feelings of hundreds of young men in this city? Like many others, I am from a dear old Christian home in the country, and when I first came to the city about twenty years ago, I abhorred sin. Gradually, I came to tolerate it, then embraced it. It is with remorse and shame that I think now of the wasted years of corruptness, of the cruel sorrow I caused my dear patient mother, whose hands were so lately folded in death, and whose prayers were constantly ascending to heaven for me. Oh sir, tell the young men not to wait until their mother's lips have grown cold to tell her that they love her, and that her Savior will be their Savior too. I wish I could warn them from my own sad experience to avoid sin and resist temptation, but sin has made a coward of me. I ask your prayers for more courage and strength."

If there is a suggestion of a disposition on the part

15

of ministers to give even the appearance of excusing sin or treating it lightly or with indifference, that very fact will alienate from the preachers many of their hearers because they know too well what sin is, and what it can do. If one would be successful in fishing for men, I would earnestly advise that his message be plain and pointed, and that no room be left for any-one to imagine that the speaker for a moment fails to recognize the awful foe with which he and the men before him have to deal. The beginnings of sin are so insidious that we cannot speak too plainly even about questionable things.

In a men's meeting, recently conducted by one of the most successful pastors in Ohio, a converted gambler and ex-saloonkeeper made the following statement, which created a profound impression. He said,

I have been in the saloon business, with a gambling room attached, for the last four years, and claim to know something about what I am now going to tell you. I do not believe that the gambling den is nearly so dangerous, nor does it do anything like the same amount of harm as the social card party in the home. I give this as my reason: In the gambling room the windows are closed tight, the curtains are pulled down, everything is conducted secretly for fear of detection, and none but gamblers, as a rule, enter there. While in the parlor, all have access to the game, children are permitted to watch it, and young people are invited to partake in it. It is made attractive and alluring by giving prizes, serving refreshments, and adding high social enjoyments. For my part, I never could see the difference between playing for a piece of silver molded in the shape of money, and silver molded in the shape of a cup or a thimble. The principle is the same, and whenever property changes hands over the luck of the cards, no matter how small the value of the prize is, I believe it is gambling.

Perhaps you have never thought of it, but where do all the gamblers come from? They are not taught in the gambling dens. A "greener," unless he is a fool, never enters a gambling hell, because he knows that he will be fleeced out of everything he possesses in less than fifteen minutes. He has learned somewhere else before he sets foot inside of such a place. When he has played in the parlor, in the social game of the home, and has become proficient enough to win prizes among his friends, the next step with him is to seek out the gambling room, for he has learned and now counts upon his ability to hold his own. The saloon men and gamblers chuckle and smile when they read in the papers of the parlor games given by the ladies, for they know that after awhile those same men will become the patrons of their business. I say, then, the parlor game is the college where gamblers are made and educated. In the name of God, men, stop this business in your homes. Burn up your decks and wash your hands.

The other day I overheard two ladies talking on the street. One said, "I am going to have a card party, and am going to the store to buy a pack of cards. Which is the best kind to get?" The other replied, "Get the Angel card. It has an angel on the back." Think of dragging the pure angels of heaven into this hellish business!

After he had taken his seat, another converted ex-gambler arose and said, "I endorse every word that the brother before me has just uttered. I was a gambler. I learned to play cards, not in the saloon, not in my own home, but in the houses of my young friends, who invited me to play with them and taught me how." A number of men went home from that afternoon meeting and set up a new rule in their families, that never should another game be played in their homes, and that their parlors should not become kindergartens for training young gamblers.

It really is an inspiration to preach to men because there is so much in a man that appeals to you – his unselfishness, his bigheartedness, his willingness to do for others, and the heroic element in him all stirs us to our best effort on his behalf.

It really is an inspiration to preach to men.

Not long ago, the country was thrilled with the news of the narrow escape from destruction of one of our great war vessels. There was a fire on board, and it was sweeping down toward the powder magazine, when almost miraculously the vessel was saved. The credit for saving the battleship *Missouri* from destruction and hundreds of her crew from death belongs to a gunner's mate named Monson. This is the report that came from Pensacola by way of Washington:

When the charge exploded in the battleship's turret, Monson was in the handling room below. He was getting out more powder from the open magazine. When fire came pouring down the ammunition hoist, Monson knew instantly what must be done. It was to shut the magazine, lest the tons of powder in it also explode and sink the ship. If Monson had stayed in the handling room, he would undoubtedly have failed to close the magazine. He would have been killed, as were his comrades there, by the explosion of the powder already taken out of the magazine. His thought and action were instant. He did the thing to be done and did it in the only way in which it could be done. He jumped into the magazine and pulled the door shut behind him. He did this in the face of certain death by fire if he failed, and probable death by water if he succeeded. For he knew that the first thing his comrades elsewhere would do would be to flood the magazine. Monson was up to his neck in water and nearly dead from suffocation. But he saved the ship and hundreds of her crew.

Gunner's mate Monson is a hero of the useful type, the hero of disciplined intelligence, the man who is not only fearless but who also thinks straight, acts fast, and so meets the requirements of a great emergency; the kind of man who, according to his opportunities, saves a ship or a nation.

It is an awful thing to realize that sin can overtake one possessed of such a spirit as this, destroy his manhood, weaken his character, blight his reputation, and cause him to lose his soul. This fact in itself should stir ministers and Christian workers to the best effort on behalf of the men around them. It is inspiring to know that we have a gospel that never fails in its power to restore lost manhood, to prevent the destruction of character, and to make possible a reputation that shall commend the owner to the favor of men and save the soul for time and for eternity.

Not long ago, there came to my notice the story of the great Seaham coal-mine explosions in England. Elderly men still live in the vicinity of this awful tragedy whose memories keep a vivid impression of that direful day. The story of the heroic death of the Christian miners is still willingly told to all who will listen.

The men were working in four gangways, striking out at right angles from a central space into which they all rushed at the first warning of danger. Then the frightful explosion took place, blocking up each of the outlets with falling stones and timbers, thus cutting off those poor imprisoned men from hope of rescue so completely that it was twelve months before the working party of excavators could reach this death trap.

When finally the dense mass of debris was dug through and cleared away, the miners came upon a gruesome scene. All of their missing mates were grouped there, as skeletons on which the clothes hung loosely, each in a sitting posture of perfect composure. The immediate cause of death was the noxious suffocating gas, in which life cannot possibly exist for any length of time. Thomas Cole, the overman, a pronounced and consistent Christian, had evidently been the last to succumb to the fatal vapor. As each of his comrades passed out of life, he had, with singular thoughtfulness, written their name and attached it to their clothes. So, when the remains were reverently and tenderly conveyed to the funeral home, each mourning family could have the poor comfort of burying their own dead.

There was another use of Thomas Cole's bit of charcoal, which cast a radiant light over the scene of death. Close to his body was a piece of paper on which was scrawled the words, "We have had a prayer meeting. Every soul ready for glory. Hallelujah! Thomas Cole."

Let us try for a moment to realize the scene. In the midst of their work, an ominous warning of catastrophe came, a sudden rush to the nearest outlet, which was the central square already described, followed by an explosion violent enough to smash down all the supports of the passages and block them with the ruins. For a moment, the men, gathered together in a position of comparative safety, would be full of thankfulness that they had escaped mutilation or a crushed-out life, but very quickly they would realize that this inside position, with the long, blocked-up passage between them and the approach of a rescue party, made their case hopeless. Then they would know, as only dying men can know, the full blessing of Christ's salvation. There would be no time for reasoning, only for a solemn renewal of faith in a living, present Savior, with earnest words of prayer and committal to Him of their wives and children who were so soon to be widows and orphans.

We know He did not fail them; we are sure He was there, and that, tenderly as a mother soothes her child in a good-night lullaby, He would hush them one by one into the sleep of death. When they woke, it would be to find that they were still with Him, but in the morning of eternal day! This was the explanation of the tranquil attitude, and of Thomas Cole's written words of final triumph. It is one more grand testimony to the surpassing excellence of our holy religion. Man may scoff at the Christian faith; it is exceedingly easy to do that. But let those laugh who win.

There is something in man that causes him to center his affections and interests with enthusiasm and untiring zeal upon whatever is before him as a goal. If he gives himself to sin, it is with terrific abandonment. If he sets out to win the favor of men, he is disposed to accomplish it at any cost. If he has decided upon amassing a fortune, he will toil day and night that his aim may be reached. It is to all such that Jesus Christ speaks when He says, *"What will it profit a man if he gains the whole world and forfeits his soul?"* (Matthew 16:26).

Count Leo Tolstoy, in one of his interesting books, tells the story of the legend of Russia, in which it was said that in a certain part of Russia a man could have all the land he could measure out from sunrise to sunset, but he must run around it all to justify his claim. He pictures one starting at sunrise and bending every energy running around his desired possession. He sees the waving trees in the distance, and determining they shall be his, he takes them in, in his race. He catches a glimpse of the shining river ahead and, putting forth renewed effort, he says, "That shall be mine," and he includes it in his circle. When, lifting his eyes to his amazement, he finds that the sun has passed the meridian, then bending every energy, he hastens back only to find that he seems to be too far away to reach the place from which he started in time to claim his possession. He runs with the speed of the wind, going faster and faster until at last, with one heroic effort, he reaches the starting place and touches the goal. All that he has encircled is his. He falls upon his face from sheer exhaustion, and when they stoop to pick him up, he is dead. He has gained it all and lost his life.

Is not this a true picture of the efforts constantly being put forth by many men today to amass a fortune or to secure honor, and is there no danger that the same sad ending will be the result? Because of the intenseness of man's nature, therefore, and because of the fact that he longs for something on which he may center his affections and consume his zeal, what an inspiration it is to the preacher to know that he may present Christ to all such. And he may also present to all such the Savior whose

There is no work in all the world so fascinating as the work in the interest of men.

presence is not only able to save from sin's penalty and sin's power, but is also able to draw out the best that is in man, until with character completely transformed, he stands ready for life in its best sense and has made provision not only for time, but for eternity as well.

There is no work in all the world so fascinating as the work in the interest of men, and he who preaches the gospel is missing almost the best of his ministry if he does not seek to become a fisher of men.

CHAPTER THREE

AN EASY WORK

S trange as it may seem, it is the universal testimony of those who have given special attention to work in the interests of men, that the easiest person in all the world to reach with the gospel is not a woman, nor a boy, nor a girl, but a man, a full-grown man, even one that is steeped in sin. I am quite well aware that very many will take exception to this statement, but I make it not only as expressing the views of others, but also as my own clear and honest conviction. But if we would have our efforts crowned with success, it is essential that we should keep in mind several great principles, the first of which is that in order to lead a man to Christ, you must first of all make him *think*. Men are so held by the power of the world, their attention is so occupied with the battle of life, and sometimes, alas, their eyes are so blinded, and their minds so deceived by the fascination of sin, that a sharp message is often needed to provoke attention. But when once their interest is aroused and the gospel is presented, it is comparatively easy to lead the impressed one to the saving knowledge of Jesus Christ.

Not long ago, at the evangelistic meetings in Chicago, a young man with a very white face came up to me saying, "What do you mean, sir, by telling my story?" And I said to him, "I do not understand you." "Well," he said, "I came into the meeting a little late, and you were using an illustration concerning a young man who had defaulted, and was trying in every way to escape arrest and elude the officers. What you said was exactly my story and I was confident that someone had discovered me and given you the account of my wrongdoing." "My dear sir," I said, "I have never seen you before; I did not even know that you were in existence," but his intense conviction was an illustration of what I have already been saying.

When the truth is presented with emphasis and plainness, it always grips, for while I had been giving the account of this particular sin of which the young man was guilty, without having him in mind, I had closed by saying, "*He who conceals his transgressions will not prosper*" (Proverbs 28:13), and "*Be sure your sin will find you out*" (Numbers 32:23). I also said, "You cannot hide away from God, and it is nearly impossible in these days for you to hide away from men." When a few days had passed, I received from him the following brief note: "Dear sir, I have resolved to take your advice and I am now going back to Cleveland to tell the truth about everything. Good-bye and God bless you."

One of my friends was preaching in a southern city

when the sheriff of the county was almost persuaded to become a Christian. The meetings closed and he had not reached a decision. A year afterward, my friend went into that city again and found that the old sheriff was dying and unsaved. He stood by his bedside holding his hand, saying, "Mr. Sheriff, they tell me you are going to die," and before he could say more, the old man drew away his hand. His face flushed and his eyes fairly flashed as he said, "Yes sir, I am going to die, and I want you to know that I am not afraid to die. I have stood face-to-face with death too many times to flinch now."

Christ is the only Savior of men.

They say he had been one of the bravest soldiers in the Confederate Army. My friend then said to him, "I am sure you are speaking the truth, and that you are not afraid to meet the great enemy we call death, but I have one question to put to you: How about the judgment, your meeting with God, and your standing face-to-face with your sins?" The old man was startled for a moment, then covering his eyes with his hands, his thin lips were seen to tremble, and the tears started to roll down his cheeks, as he said, "God pity me, sir, I am not ready for the judgment." The one thing that moved him was the sharp question of the minister, and what is true in conversation will be equally true in preaching.

It is likewise necessary for us to remember that Christ is the only Savior of men, and that if men have rejected Christ, then according to the Scriptures they are lost. This is not an easy thing to say, but it must be said if we accept the Bible as the word of God. Clearly must it be shown that the chief of all sins is the rejection of the Son of God. When Jesus spoke concerning the coming of the Holy Spirit, He said, *"And He, when He comes, will convict the world concerning sin"* (John 16:8), and the word *convict* is a judicial expression, which means to set before or make plain, as a lawyer sets before the jury the evidence against the one who is accused. But in this instance, Jesus clearly states that the sin of which the Spirit of God will convict men is that they have not believed in the Son of God. When the day of judgment comes, therefore, the question that will be asked is not, "Were you drunken or profane, dishonest or impure?" but, "What did you do with Jesus Christ?" Upon the answer to that question depends our standing or falling in the presence of the judge on the great white throne.

It must also be remembered that there is no work so delicate as the work of winning souls, and this is especially true when attention is given to the winning of men. I once heard Dr. Talmage say in his characteristic fashion, "There is no art quite so fine as that of the fisherman." Jesus knew exactly what He was talking about and what He had in mind for His disciples when He said, *"I will make you fishers of men."* When a true fisherman fishes in these days, he selects the most delicate rod, equips it with the finest line, and puts upon it the most tempting fly. He then wades, carefully and as far as possible, noiselessly into the stream. With a dexterous throw, he casts his line and almost instantly has in his basket a beautiful trout, which is the sure reward of his fisher's skill. "But" says Dr. Talmage, "when we attempt to fish for men, we do exactly the opposite. We use a beam for a rod, a cable for a line, and an anchor for a hook, and then with great commotion, we cast out into the great sea of life and say to men, 'Bite or be damned.'"

"Is it any wonder," said the great preacher, "that we are so unsuccessful when we have so far missed the thought of the greatest of all fishers for men, even Jesus Christ Himself?"

Again, we must be wedded to no particular method to be successful in our work. There are some men who seem to be staunchly opposed to anything that suggests variety or change. And yet Jesus was rarely twice the same. He talked quietly in one place and lifted up His voice to cry aloud in another. He pleaded upon the mountainside and stretched forth His hands in an appeal from Peter's boat. He spoke tenderly to little children and the mothers that bore them into His presence, and cried aloud in another instance, saying to men who mocked Him, *"You brood of vipers, how will you escape the sentence of hell?"* (Matthew 23:33).

He used all kinds of illustrations: today a crystal of salt, and tomorrow a grain of mustard seed. In this sermon the flowers were His illustration, and in the next the flying birds carried home His message of truth. The apostle Paul also gloried in the fact that he could be all things to all men, if by all means he might save some (1 Corinthians 9:22). We, therefore, in these modern times, need not be afraid of change and variety, for we have illustrious examples before us.

While vacationing one time on the shores of Lake

George, I was told by an old fisherman that if I would rise early in the morning, row across the lake, and anchor my boat at a certain point, I could catch any number of fish and almost any kind that I desired. I eagerly awaited the coming of the day, rowed across the bay, anchored my boat as I had been told, and cast my line repeatedly, never once getting a bite. At last, in sheer disgust, I was lifting my anchor, when this same old fisherman rowed up by my side and dropped his anchor, making rapid preparations to fish. I saw him cast his line and draw it in very soon without a fish, and very naturally I was pleased. Then I saw him bend down for a moment in the bottom of his boat, work very quickly with his hands, cast his line the second time, and instantly draw in as fine a fish as one could hope to catch in inland waters. "How in the world did you do it?" I said to him. And without stopping a moment in his work, in characteristic fisher fashion he said, "I just changed my bait."

It is hardly possible for one man to duplicate another's work.

This is sometimes very necessary in our fishing for men. If one thing will not win them, then let us try another. If one method fails, without in the least being discouraged, let us adopt another method and keep on changing, if that be necessary, until at last we have a method of which God can approve and which through us He may be able to use. It is hardly possible for one man to duplicate another's work. The same spirit may possess them both, and yet while the method is

30

different, the results may be practically the same, and that is the important thing.

Again, if we are expecting to be used of God to win men to Christ, let us begin with those nearest to our own hands. If you are a minister, then evangelize your own people first. If you are a businessman, lead your own children, your own employees, or your own friends first, remembering this: not until we fill the narrow circle in which we live and work will God lead us out into the broader sphere.

A gentleman came up to one of my friends recently and said, "I have about decided to enter upon evangelistic work, and I want you to make a few suggestions to me. I have decided upon my field. I shall go into Colorado or California, and I am very sure that with such a class of people as I will find there, I shall be successful." My friend said to him, "Do you live here?" and the gentleman said, "Yes sir, with my brother and sisters."

"Then may I ask you this question: Is your brother a Christian?"

"Well, no," he said, "he is not. The fact is, I have never asked him."

"May I ask if your sisters are Christians?"

"No," he said, "they are not, for as a matter of fact, we are not on very good terms with each other, and I know little about their spiritual condition."

Then my friend turned on him sharply and said, "God will never use you, sir, in the broader work until you are successful in your home field." Build your own house first, and then you may expect God to want you elsewhere.

And finally, if one is to be used of God in winning men, he must give the strictest attention to his own personal life, his habits, and his character. As the old hymn goes,

> Thou must be true thyself,
>> If thou another soul wouldst reach,
> It needs the overflow of heart
>> To give the lips full speech.

The least touch with the world robs us of power. The unconfessed sin will take the ring out of our testimony. A miserable disposition will undo all that we could say to others even though Jesus Christ Himself may be the theme of our conversation. There is one prayer that every Christian worker ought to offer at the beginning of and throughout his life of service: *Search me, O God, and know my heart; try me and know my anxious thoughts; and see if there be any hurtful way in me* (Psalm 139:23-24). God does not require either golden vessels or silver vessels for His use, but He must have vessels that are clean. If we are covering any sin in our lives, this will be a barrier to the manifestation of divine grace, and this thought is placed last, in order that it may come with special emphasis. When all the above suggestions have been clearly understood, then it would be well for us to wait before God and say, "And now, my Father, I am willing to do or to be anything, only use me." I expect that the experience of the poet is ours:

The strong man's strength to toil for Christ,
The fervent preacher's skill,
I sometimes wish, but better far,
To be just what God wills;
No service in itself is small,
None great though earth it fill,
But that is small which seeks its own,
That great which seeks God's will.

CHAPTER FOUR

PERSONAL EVANGELISM FOR MEN

However much emphasis may be placed upon the public preaching of the gospel, or however much importance we may attach to general evangelistic meetings, after all, personal evangelism is the most important part of all our work. At this particular time in the church's history, it calls for special attention. It is not difficult to approach men regarding their relation to Christ and eternity, if first one lives a consistent life, and then, as has been previously stated, has a perfectly natural way of presenting the claims of the Son of God. For in these days, no man has a right to be indifferent to Christ who is the central figure of all history, who is God's revelation to man, and who is man's best friend in every emergency of his life.

You need not fear rebuff. I have been for fifteen years interested in the special work for men. Naturally, I have spoken to very many about coming to Christ. In all that time, I have had but one rebuff. One cold, stormy day, up in the northern part of the state of New York, accompanied by one of my church officers, I drove ten miles to ask a gentleman to become a Christian and to unite with the church. Two members of his family expected to identify themselves with us, and it seemed an opportune time to approach the husband and father. The thermometer registered twenty degrees below zero, and literally in an almost-frozen condition I reached the farmer's house, met him halfway between his barn and his house, and approached him at once stating the intent of my visit. "I have come," I said, "to ask you to be a Christian and to join the church." With flushed face and blazing eyes he said, "Well, sir, I want you to attend to your own business, and when I want you to speak to me on this matter, I will send for you, and until I do, please stay away." Without inviting me into his house, he turned away from me. I stepped into the cold wind and drove back ten miles through the storm, reaching my home almost insensible from the cold. My visit seemed a failure.

Ten years afterwards, to the very month and almost to the very day, I was preaching in the First Methodist Church in Saratoga Springs, when a man rose in the audience, saying, "Please pray for me." When he thought I did not see him, he stepped out into the aisle and began walking towards the front of the church. Then facing the great audience, he said, "Ten years ago, I insulted this minister when he came to me to ask me to be a Christian. When I entered my house, my daughter, who had heard my remark, threw her arms around my neck and said, 'Oh Father, will there never be another chance?' I have prayed to God to let me live long enough to confess Christ in this minister's presence; I do it now, and I bear testimony to this fact that never in all my life was I so profoundly moved as when he spoke to me that winter day." And so, my journey, after all, was not a failure.

I am making no plea for what may seem to be anything like fanaticism, but rather just for consistency on the part of Christian men in their responsibility for other people. A Christian banker in a Pennsylvania city noticed that two young men in the bank, after business hours, were accustomed to the use of profanity. He called them into his office and said, "Gentlemen, I am a Christian, I am responsible for this banking house, and so long as I am, you cannot be profane. What you do outside of the bank, I am not able to control, but what you do here I am certainly accountable for. May I ask you," he said, "where you are living?" and they told him they were living in boardinghouses in the city, their homes being elsewhere. "Then may I ask you," he said, "as your friend, how you spend your evenings, and if your mothers are living?" That question brought tears to their eyes.

"Now gentlemen," he said, "I do not want to appeal to your emotions, but no man can be at his best in these days and disregard the claims of Jesus Christ. The only manly life to live is the Christian life." Then he dismissed them from his presence. The next morning, one of these young men entered his office to say, "I want to thank you for your conversation. Last night I began to read my Bible again and I bowed my knees in prayer." Such a conversation as this is the thing for which I plead, for this should be the spirit of Christian businessmen. Thousands of young men could be kept from wandering and thousands more could be won to Christ.

One reason why we win so few people in these days is because we are so unbusinesslike in our approach to men. One of the bishops of the Methodist Church told me of a young Methodist minister who, entering upon one of his first pastorates, with the assistance of one of his elders, made a list of businessmen who ought to be identified with his church. In a perfectly businesslike manner, he visited them. He entered one bank, and said to the bank president, "Sir, I am the pastor of the Methodist Church, and a minister of Jesus Christ. At your convenience, I would like to talk with you about your soul, and I have come to ask you to make an appointment with me." The hour set was four o'clock the next day. Before the minister had left the banking house after his second visit, he had won the banker to Christ. I am persuaded that this spirit would win in many instances.

One of my friends, beginning a new pastorate, determined to speak personally to everyone in his congregation about their soul's welfare. He approached his organist first and asked him if he was a Christian and, to his amazement, found out that he was not, and yet he had spent twenty-five years playing the organ in different churches. "Would you mind telling me frankly why you are not?" said my friend, and the answer given with tears was this: "With the exception of my mother, you are the only person in all my life that has ever asked me to be a Christian. I thank you for your interest, and I will give the subject my attention." In less than two weeks, he was a professed follower of Jesus Christ and a member of the church.

I am sure that many of us are failing in our work just here. We let opportunities for speaking to others slip away from us, and while we are busy with trifling things, souls pass into eternity, alas, unsaved.

As I journeyed on the train the other day, traveling westward, I saw in the section opposite my own a woman who was weeping bitterly. I crossed over to her and said, "I am a minister, and if I can serve you in any way, it would be my pleasure." I learned that her husband, from whom she had been separated on a visit,

We let opportunities for speaking to others slip away from us.

had suddenly taken ill. She was hurrying from New York to her Colorado home, hoping to see him before he died. In Chicago, she had received the message that he was dead, and she seemed well-nigh heartbroken. Among other things, I asked her if her husband was a Christian. She told me he was not. Then later she said that formerly he was a member of a church, but in his Western home where he had lived for twenty-five years, he had never united with the church. I asked her if he knew any minister personally, and she said, "Oh yes, one of them used to frequently visit him. They talked and laughed about various matters, but my husband used to come home very often and say, 'I wonder why he never asks me to enter his church. I would be so glad if he would.'" And I said to her, "Do you think he would have responded favorably?" and then with a sob she answered, "My husband and I have been ready for years to enter the church, but no one in our Western home has ever invited us." This is a solemn charge to bring against the church, but alas, in too many instances it is a just charge.

There are many ways by means of which we could win men to Christ.

First. Speak to them personally. One good rule is this: Whenever you have an impression that you ought to speak to anyone about his soul, go at once to follow your leading. As a rule, it is true that when God moves you to go, He is moving another to receive you. The proverb says, *Like apples of gold in settings of silver is a word spoken in right circumstances* (Proverbs 25:11).

Second. If you are unable to speak, then write a letter, praying its truth will be received as you write, and commit it to God that He may work through it. Not long ago I met, personally, the chief justice of the supreme court of one of our western states. I learned from his own lips, and later from the minister who had been instrumental in his conversion, the story of his coming to Christ. He was a brilliant lawyer, but unsaved, and the minister became greatly concerned for him. He was afraid to speak to him because of his prominent position, so he wrote a letter to him, but before he could mail it, his courage failed him, and he tore it up. Then his wife came to the rescue and said, "Write another letter and we will pray earnestly about it." The letter was written and a little booklet by Charles Spurgeon was slipped into it. The letter was carried to the chief justice, and they waited eagerly for a reply. Soon it came in the justice's own handwriting. "My dear Sir: Your kind letter and the little book have been received and read. I have been waiting for this message for fifteen years, and I write to tell you that because of your appeal I have given myself to Jesus Christ." In many days, I have not met a more devoted, loyal Christian than the chief justice of the supreme court of this western state.

Third. If you desire to win a soul to Christ, whether you speak or write, by all means pray. We have come to a time when we are quite disposed to think of prayer as spent force. In a great city the other day, my own faith was mightily strengthened in prayer. A man came to speak to me, boasting of his infidelity. His remarks were so blasphemous that I threatened to leave him, and with a half-spoken apology he told me that his boy was dangerously ill. I think that God was going to use that conviction for his conversion. At a noonday business meeting following my interview, the following request was placed in my hands: "Kindly at noon today have your Christian hearers join with you in prayer for the sick son of an unbelieving father who cannot pray, and makes the request at the asking of a prayerful Christian wife." This son was dying of pleuropneumonia. When the father had left the home in the morning, the case seemed hopeless. Just before noon, the physician gave up all hope. His temperature was beyond the danger

41

point and, humanly speaking, he was practically hopeless. Between twelve and half past twelve o'clock, seven hundred men bowed in prayer, and Major James H. Cole rose to voice our petitions. He prayed as I never heard him pray before. It seemed as if the windows to heaven were truly open above us. Here is the answer to his prayer: Between half past twelve and one o'clock, the boy's condition suddenly changed, and his temperature miraculously dropped to normal. When the physician came in, expecting to find him dead, the boy had passed the danger point and his recovery was made by leaps and bounds. The following Sunday, that father stood in a meeting for men, saying, with great emotion, "I have been an unbeliever and have blasphemed God, but today I desire to say that I want to know the God that has answered your prayers for my boy, and so far as I know the way, I will yield myself to Him." Step by step, he has come out into an ever-brightening Christian experience.

Does it not seem easy to be a soul winner?

Does it not seem easy to be a soul winner? It is not simply given to those who are rich or wise or great in the estimation of men, but the work is for everyone who will truly live for Christ and honestly feel a burden of responsibility for others.

While preaching in New York recently, my attention was repeatedly drawn to a gentleman who, with his wife, was present at almost every service. I learned afterwards that the wife was a Christian, and that her husband was an honest inquirer. The last evening of one of the meetings, I was preaching on the text of John 3:3: *Jesus answered and said to him, "Truly, truly, I say to you, unless one is born* *again he cannot see the kingdom of God."* At the close of the service, this gentleman deliberately rose and clearly and definitely accepted Christ as his Savior. The next afternoon, I was preaching in a neighboring church. Just as I was passing out of the service, I was asked to stop and meet a little boy. I noticed that he was lame, and his face bore not only the marks of suffering but also had that peculiar expression that belongs to one who is almost nearer to heaven than earth. Some illness had made it necessary to amputate one of his legs, and leaning on his crutches, he said to me, "I am so glad that my father came to Christ," and then the minister told me the story of the gentleman whose decision had been made the night before.

When the meetings began, this little boy had insisted that his mother should see to it that his father was present at every service. He said, "I cannot go, I know, but while you are with him in the meeting, I will pray." Each night when the parents entered the door, the child's first inquiry would be as to the father's acceptance of Christ. One evening, it was raining furiously in the city, and the father had determined to stay at home, but at the boy's urgent plea he went to the church, with the result that I have mentioned previously, namely, his conversion. That night, when they came home, the boy said to him, "You need not tell me, for I know what you have done." The little fellow said to me, "I never would have given up on him so long as I lived." When the father came to bid me good-bye at the last service, he said, "I want to thank you for your words spoken to me in the sermon, but I am compelled to say that the earnest prayer and the unwavering faith of my lame boy forced me to do what I did, and I never can fully express my pleasure at the result of this new stand that I have taken."

So you see, it is not necessary that we should be great or strong to be winners of souls if our lives are right and our prayers are as they should be. We can win to the Savior those for whom we are concerned, and that is not only joy here, but also throughout eternity.

If I could know that word or deed
Of mine had helped a soul in need,
Had given comfort, eased the smart
Of some poor, tortured, aching heart,
With what rare joy my heart would glow,
If I could know! If I could know!

If one should whisper in my ear,
"Your words have made me stronger, sir,
To fight this evil thing within,
That leads me often into sin"—
Life's darkened ways would brighter grow,
If I could know! If I could know!

Each day I ask the Lord to bless
Some act of mine to fruitfulness,
And though I know not how or where
He sends the answer to my prayer,
When I into His presence go,
Then I shall know! Then I shall know!

CHAPTER FIVE

HOW SOME MEN HAVE BEEN WON TO CHRIST

O ne reason why so many people in the church have been unsuccessful in Christian work is that they make it too difficult a matter. One ought to work for Christ as he plays golf, that is, with perfect freedom. No muscle should be tense with the golf player. There must be perfect rhythm in all his actions. This is a simple illustration of the spirit of Christian work, yet a true one. Nothing that resembles jargon and nothing that even hints at the unnatural should for a moment be expected to win in the turning of lost men to Christ. Do your work in the easiest way. Talk about your Savior in the most natural fashion. Present Him to your friends as your best friend. Show by your countenance that He is even more than you claim He is. All this must be backed up by consistent Christian living, and there will be little question of real success in the effort.

There are, as a rule, many forces behind the one on whose behalf we labor. Of these, we do well to take advantage.

The influence of a mother counts for more than any human power. In the presence of a great audience of men recently, I asked this question: "How many here came to Christ as a direct or indirect result of a mother's influence?" and two-thirds of the Christian men in the audience immediately sprang to their feet to testify to the power of the holy living and consistent working of their mothers, many of whom had passed over on the other shore. A group of rough miners in Leadville, Colorado, gave me a respectful hearing, but rather an indifferent one, until I casually mentioned a mother's love. Instantly there was a change in the facial expression of almost every man present, and here and there tears were being brushed away from hardened faces as the picture of their mothers passed before them. In a successful men's meeting, conducted by Dr. Alderson in his own church, a traveling man, quite young in years, arose and told, very modestly and feelingly, the following pathetic story:

Before I left home to go on the road, I had fallen into many bad habits, which gave my Christian mother great concern and anxiety. She feared the result upon my life after I got beyond the influence of my home and came into contact with the gambler's temptations. I was a cardplayer and very fond of the amusement. I knew that many gamblers spent their leisure evenings at the hotel and saloon card table, for I had myself often played with them when they stopped overnight in our town. I felt that one of the first requisites of a traveling man's outfit was a pack of cards. So, the afternoon before I was to leave home, I purchased a brand-new deck and went to bed that night leaving them in my coat pocket.

The next morning, I started on the road. Just as I was leaving home my mother kissed me, then laid her face against my cheek, and in a few words pleaded with me to be a good boy and not forget my Christian home. I felt her warm tears flow down my cheek.

The first night out found me in Winchester, Kentucky. Meeting several traveling men during the day, we agreed to put up at the same hotel, and after supper spend the evening with cards. When the time came, as we were seated around the table, one of the men asked, "Who has got a pack of cards?" Quickly I responded, "I've got the cards all right." Thrusting my hand into my coat pocket I pulled out a little package wrapped exactly as I had put it into my pocket the day before, and just about the same size. Unwrapping it in the presence of the others, with all eyes fixed upon my action, what was my astonishment and mortification to find instead of cards a copy of the New Testament, which my mother, sometime in the small hours of the night, had dexterously substituted for my cards. I blushed and apologized and confessed to my friends. We were all deeply affected. My dear mother broke me not only of playing cards, but she has been the means of bringing me to Christ, and whenever now I am tempted to do wrong, I can feel the hot tears of my mother trickling down my face.

The influence of a father is not to be forgotten. Too frequently in paying tribute to a mother's devotion do we forget to pay our respects to the consistent living and the faithful working of the Christian fathers of our land. "How did you come to Christ?" said one minister to another. The quick response was: "My father's wrestling for us at the family altar did it. He used to call us by name in his prayers, and I never could get away from his praying." "And how did you come to faith?" was asked of another, and the answer given was: "It was the evening of the day on which my mother was buried, and we children, with our brokenhearted father, were sitting in the log house on the frontier before a blazing fire.

I saw my father cutting away a small piece of wood and was interested to see that he had fashioned a cross that he could hold between his thumb and finger. Then holding it up before us in the flickering light, he told us the story of Jesus Christ cradled in a manger, living in Nazareth, preaching in Galilee, suffering in the garden, and dying on just such a cross as he held up before us. In an impassioned way, he called us to our mother's Savior and because of his own holy living, that night every child came to Christ."

I would like to pay tribute to my own father's devotion to his children in this connection. As a motherless boy, temptations came upon me thick and fast. My father one day called me to his side and said, "My son, I have always tried to live as I should before you.

If in any way I have failed, I beg your pardon and ask your forgiveness. May I say to you, my boy, that if you ever disgrace your father's name, and are unworthy of your angel-mother's love, you will kill me." One night there came to me a sharp, sudden temptation to do at least a questionable thing. I started down the street of the city where I then lived, when suddenly, as I came to a street corner, and was just about to turn into the way that would, I believe, have inevitably meant death, there came up before me the words of my father, and I think that I am a minister today because of a father's devotion to his children and his earnest desire to hold us for Christ.

While preaching in Chicago, a young man was most joyfully converted. He was a graduate of a southern college and had been admitted to the bar as a lawyer, but while giving every evidence of achieving success in his work, he was restless, dissatisfied, and in great danger of being wrecked morally. In our meeting, I used the illustration of Jonah attempting to go to Tarshish when God wanted him to proceed to Nineveh, and I said that because of this, everything was against him. This brought the young man to a realization of his condition. He saw where he was drifting, realized why it was that he had been so disturbed and distressed, and by an act of his will he stepped out of almost-midnight darkness into the clear light of the knowledge of God.

The next day, he gave this touching testimony in the presence of a great number of men: "Gentlemen," he said, "I have had peace and blessing during the last twenty-four hours, but may I say that I believe the only thing that has influenced my life during these years of my wandering and kept me back from doing many a thing that I might otherwise have done has been the memory of my father." Then he drew from his pocket his father's picture, and holding it up he said, shaking with great emotion, "This is my father's picture. I always have thought it the noblest and best picture in the world. He has been dead for five years, and during all that time this face has haunted me. I knew that he wanted me to be a Christian and preach the gospel, but I hesitated and grieved him inexpressibly. During all these years, I could not get away from his look. But during the past twenty-four hours, everything has been changed. I am now looking towards that day when I shall see him once again with that happy smile once more upon his features, for I have determined to preach the gospel."

These are but a few illustrations. They could be multiplied indefinitely. Given a boy with a true mother and a noble father, both of them Christians, there is every reason to believe that the ultimate winning of that boy to Christ will be almost absolutely certain.

The experiences through which men pass are not to be lost sight of when attempting to win them to Jesus Christ. The loss of a mother, an experience in sickness, the sudden accident that almost meant death – these things are as a rule to be taken into account when we attempt to win the lost to Him.

One of my best friends in New York, an honored officer of a strong church, once told me this story that aptly illustrates my point. He said, "When I was a boy

of about twelve years of age, I went with my parents
and a brother who was two years older than me, to
spend the summer vacation at a lake in the northern
part of the state of New York. This lake was like home
to me, for from my earliest infancy my family had
been spending the summers there. My brother and I
had been in the habit of going out on the lake to fish,
but always accompanied by an older person. The day
that I am writing about I shall never forget.

"My brother and I had been more than anxious
to go fishing by ourselves. With boyhood's enthusiasm, we believed if allowed to do so, we would show
what wonderful fishermen we really were, and would
return with a string of fish that would fairly astonish
our parents and the other guests of the hotel where
we were staying. After numerous pleadings, our father
had finally given his consent, with the distinct promise
on our part that whenever it became necessary for us
to change seats, we would first take the boat ashore
before attempting to do so, and on no account would
we stand up in the boat.

"The eventful day finally arrived, and bright and
early, with our poles, tackle, and bait, we got into our
boat and started out. We kept our promise that we had
made, not to stand up in the boat, and all went well.
The time came for us to return, and as my brother
rowed the boat back to the hotel, we discovered that
during our absence an old barge, loaded with wood,
had arrived and been tied up to the end of the dock. I
then forgot the promise that up to this time had been
so carefully kept, and I said to my brother, 'You row

quietly by the old barge and I will step out on it and run up to the house and let the people know we are home, and you take the boat around to the shore and put her up.' I stood up, I made a step, the boat slipped away from me, I lost my balance, and in an instant, I found myself unable to swim in twenty feet of water.

"Quickly I went to the bottom; with eyes closed from fright, I came to the surface only to sink again. I tried in every way to swim, but every effort only made my case more hopeless. I think every sin that I had committed came into my mind, and foremost was the fact that I had disobeyed my father. Presently I realized that the next time I would sink would be the last, when suddenly I heard a voice ringing in my ears, 'Catch hold of my hand.' Then my eyes were opened and I saw my brother, who had backed up the boat, leaning as far as he could over the stern of the boat and with outstretched hand trying to reach me. I caught hold of his hand, and he drew me gently towards him. Then putting his arms around me, he lifted me with such a strength as I never knew he possessed safely into the boat and took me to the shore.

"Years passed by, I grew to be a man, I married and had a family of my own. I was not a Christian; far from it. On account of my family, I was a pewholder in one of the prominent churches of New York. I had turned a deaf ear to the religious teachings of my parents. I had grown indifferent. I came to the place where I really did not care for God or man. One night, when I went home from business, I found waiting for me in my home the pastor of the church I attended. He said something like this: 'I have come to ask you if you will come up to church Monday night. We are to hold a week of special services. An evangelist is to be with us, and I want you to come.' I was angry for what I called unwarranted interference, and so I said, 'Pastor, thank you, I will promise you *not* to come. I am glad to see you on any other subject, but on this subject let me say I go to church on Sunday; on other days I want to be left alone.' How many times have I wished that I had never so spoken to him!

"Monday night came. I went home and found my wife ready to go to church. I didn't want her to go alone, neither was I willing to go, and so a compromise was made. I was to take her to the church door and call for her an hour later. She went into the service. I stood outside. It was a bitterly cold night, and at times I felt as if I would perish, and yet I would not go in. Finally, I could stand it no longer, and I decided that I would go in and take a back seat and get warm. Thank God I got warm that night, and I have been warm ever since. As the evangelist was speaking, it seemed as if he knew me. He pictured my case exactly: disobedient to God, indifferent to His Word, forgetful of the prayers and religious influence that my parents had surrounded me with in childhood.

"Then there flashed through my heart and mind the picture of my boyhood days, as I struggled in the water and I could see myself now sinking in the waves of sin, and, believing this was my last opportunity, that soon I would be lost. Then I could hear the voice of Jesus say, 'Take hold of My hand.' By faith, my eyes were opened.

I saw Him then in all His beauty and heard Him say, *'Come unto me.'* By faith I took His hand; He has put His great loving arms around me, and with a strength I never even knew my elder brother possessed, has lifted me out of my distresses and is now guiding and taking me safely to the heavenly shore.

"Some fifteen years have now passed since I found Christ. A few years ago, I visited the old lake up north. I rowed by the old dock. A similar old wooden barge was again tied up to the dock. As I told my wife and children who were with me in the boat of my narrow escape from drowning when I was a boy, I also told them of my narrow escape in later years from being lost in the waves of sin. Today we have a happy home, every member of the family is a member of God's family, and Jesus Christ is a welcome guest in our home. I have been telling the simple story of Christ's love for sinful men ever since He saved me, and I expect to tell it right along until I shall see Him face-to-face."

CHAPTER SIX

A WORD WITH THE HEAD OF THE HOUSE

For I have chosen him, so that he may command his children and his household after him. (Genesis 18:19)

Riding through the country not long ago with one of the bishops of the Methodist Church, I said to him, "What is the special truth today needing emphasis in our teaching?" He responded quickly, "A better home life." This being true, there is no one of greater importance in the consideration of this subject than the head of the household, the father, and the husband. You always do well to tie yourself to the man in whom the Lord has confidence. He loves us all and will continue to love us until the end, but He trusts only a few, it would seem. The world usually bases its opinion of us upon our reputation; God always bases His upon character. Abraham was truly a great man and a good man of whom God could say, as in the text above quoted, *For I have chosen him, so that he may command his children and his household after him.*

There are two or three things in particular in the story of Abraham that should be remembered, for they show God's appreciation of him.

First. When Lot was separated from Abraham and he stood alone, Abraham permitted God to choose for him. You can only fully trust a man who allows God this privilege.

Second. Do not forget that picture of him as he sat at the door of the tent at noon, when three men in shining garments stood before him; they were angels. The principal one was the angel of the covenant or the angel of the Lord. Happy is a man in whose home the Lord loves to stay, and in whose home there is nothing to forbid His resting for a little while. How would it be in your own home? His will is that husbands should love their wives, that wives should obey their husbands, that children should honor their parents, and that parents should not provoke their children to wrath, for He cannot remain where there is the least contention or strife. Have you noticed the question that the angel of the Lord put to Abraham? *"Where is Sarah, your wife?"* he said (Genesis 18:9). How did he know that he had a

Happy is a man in whose home the Lord loves to stay.

wife, or that her name was Sarah? For the very reason that the eyes of God are upon us always. He is taking note of all we do. He weighs our motives and reads our thoughts and numbers our households, and Abraham stood this test, so the Scripture was true of him.

Third. There is some significance in the fact that Abraham had what Lot did not have. Three angels came to him, but only two came to Lot. The angel of the covenant did not go into Sodom. Both of these men, Abraham and Lot, were God's chosen ones, but the difference was that Abraham dwelt in Canaan while Lot dwelt in the cities of the plain. We may as well remember that God only dwells with the man whose life is lived according to His will. What an illustration Christ was in this respect! *"BEHOLD, I HAVE COME TO DO YOUR WILL,"* He said (Hebrews 10:9). This was His life. *"My food is to do the will of Him who sent Me"* (John 4:34). It was His food. *"For whoever does the will of God, he is My brother and sister and mother"* (Mark 3:35). In that society He lived and lives today. *Teach me to do Your will* (Psalm 143:10). It was His whole education. *I delight to do Your will* (Psalm 40:8). It was His constant pleasure. *The one who does the will of God lives forever* (1 John 2:17). It makes provision for our eternity.

I know how much holy sentiment there is about mothers, and I would not detract in the least from it, but have you ever noticed how the Bible exalts the love of a father? When the tenderness of God is to be pictured, it is in these words: *Just as a father has compassion on his children* (Psalm 103:13); and again in the story of Jacob, when he said, *"You have bereaved me of my children"* (Genesis 42:36); and still again in the sob of David, when he cried out, *"O my son Absalom, O Absalom, my son, my son!"* (2 Samuel 19:4); or in the picture in the New Testament of the father who wailed for the prodigal to return. The records of the church have been made glorious by the stories of the faithfulness of fathers as well as the devotion of mothers.

In the autobiography of John G. Paton, the missionary to the New Hebrides, the great missionary attributed most of the blessing of his life to the influence of his father. The boy was on his way to Glasgow to begin his lifework, and he said, "My father walked with me six miles. His counsel, his tears, his heavenly conversation are as fresh as if they happened yesterday. Tears are on my cheeks as freely now as then, whenever memory steals me away to the scene. The last half-mile was walked in unbroken silence, with his hat in his hand, his long hair flowing upon his shoulders, his lips moving in silent prayer, and tears falling from his eyes when our eyes met.

Suddenly we stopped, and he said, 'God bless you, my son; may your father's God prosper you and keep you from evil.' Unable to say more, we embraced and parted. When I came to the bend in the road and looked back, I saw that he was still standing and looking, and then I climbed to the dike and looked and he was still waiting, and I vowed a vow that I would never do a thing that would disgrace such a father, and the memory of him drove me to do God's will as he did it."

It is my prayerful hope that the picture of such a

father might inspire us all. The Bible teaches that every man must be a priest in his own household. If so, he must keep himself unspotted from the world. "I charge you," said a dying mother to her husband, "to bring all these children home with you," and that is God's charge to every father in this world.

There are certain reasons why God could say of Abraham, *I know him* (Genesis 18:19 KJV). He could remember how he had been living back in Ur, or in the days of idolatry, when He called him as He afterwards called Elijah, Peter, Matthew, and still later summoned Cromwell from his farm and Luther from the cloister, when the call means separation from the fatherland and his kinsmen, and that he must be a stranger in a strange land. It is written in Hebrews: *Abraham, when he was called, obeyed* (Hebrews 11:8), and that made him a hero. God always trusts men when they obey Him, and no one can ever command until first he learns to obey. No home can be happy unless the children obey the parents, and no home can be a true home unless the parents obey God. Have you obeyed God in your home? In His sight you are a priest; have you maintained your position?

In the life of John G. Paton, we are told that the custom of morning and evening prayer was always maintained in his father's household; until the day of his death, at seventy-seven years, he failed not, and when the last day of his life came, he was heard repeating the psalm and breaking forth into prayer. His distinguished son said, "I never can remember that any day ever passed when this was omitted. No hurry for the market, no rush for business, no arrival of friends, no trouble or joy ever prevented our kneeling around the altar, while the high priest led us to God and offered himself and his children there. The worst woman in the town where we lived crept up to that window and heard my father pleading for sinners in his prayer and was saved."

Oh, for a home so full of God that the overflow of it can lead a soul to Christ! God was not shut up to the present or the past in knowing Abraham, but the future was as an open book. He knew that Abraham would stand as an intercessor for Sodom, and He knew exactly what kind of intercession that would be. It is a pattern for us today. There was real concern for Lot.

An old Scotch woman's son, Walter, had gone away and sent his mother no letter, so that she did not know whether he was dead or alive. Every night, as she prayed, she would throw open the door and cry aloud, "Come home, Walter; your mother misses you so," and every morning, for twenty years, at the break of day, she climbed to the top of the hill and looked in the direction in which he had gone and prayed for his return. Abraham's concern was like this; there was real prayer in his intercession. He waited until he was alone with God. Every father ought to have such an experience as this.

Oh, for a home so full of God that the overflow of it can lead a soul to Christ!

Referring again to the life of John G. Paton, the great missionary said, "Our house consisted of two rooms, one front and one back. There was a kind of closet between, and there, three times a day, my father retired and shut the door. We children got to understand and know by a kind of instinct that the prayer was being poured out there after the manner of the high priests in the holy of holies. We occasionally heard his pathetic tones pleading for us, and we walked past the door on tiptoe for fear we might disturb him." No wonder a home like that has blessed the world.

God also knew Abraham in that other real test of his faith when He said, *"Take now your son, your only son, whom you love, Isaac"* (Genesis 22:2). Isaac was the dearest thing in the world to him. Suppose God should touch that which is best in your life; what would you say? If anyone could rebel under such circumstances, there must be something wrong.

I can see Abraham and Isaac starting off early in the morning, for three days they journey, and then they see the mountain of sacrifice, and Abraham says, "Wait here." When Isaac asks him, saying, *"Where is the lamb?"* (Genesis 22:7), the father's reply is: "God will prepare His sacrifice." He places Isaac upon the altar, raises the knife that flashes in the sunlight, and suddenly God says, *"Do not stretch out your hand against the lad, and do nothing to him; for now I know that you fear God, since you have not withheld your son, your only son, from Me"* (Genesis 22:12). It may be that there is something between you and your children that is keeping them back from Christ.

A father and a son heard the minister preach when the subject was "The Judgment." The boy was profoundly moved and walked home from the church without saying a word, made his way to his room, threw himself upon his bed, and a little later heard his father whistling and singing. He rose from his bed and said, "It cannot be true; if my father realized that I was lost he could not whistle, and he would not sing." And when that boy came to manhood, instead of casting his influence as he might have done with the evangelical church, he became one of the greatest leaders of Unitarianism that the world has ever known. It may be that you have not yet yielded up everything you have to God, and for that reason your home life is not all that it should be. Never until spirit, soul, and body are absolutely controlled by God may we expect Him to dwell in us in fullness and use us for His glory. It may be that you are living in what may be properly called a backsliding condition; if so, then let it be ever remembered that God will not send His blessing upon you until you come back into close fellowship with Him.

I once heard Major Whittle give the following illustration: "At a weekly prayer meeting where 'Separation from the world and consecration to God' had been presented as the topic for consideration, a gentleman related the following experience:

"'I came to this city several years ago a professing Christian. I was a member of such a church, a regular attendee at the prayer meeting, a teacher in the Sunday school, and I maintained daily worship in my family. But gradually I became engrossed in business, and the ambition to be rich took possession of me. I gave up my Sunday-school class – too tired when Sunday came to attend it – and the prayer meeting was neglected for the same reason. Soon family worship was also dropped, and I went on for some years a merely nominal Christian, attending church on Sunday, but without any real communion with God, and without any real happiness of soul. God often spoke to me, and I expected His chastening hand to come in some way. At last, it came. I had but one child – a little daughter – the idol of my heart. One evening I was unexpectedly at home. My business usually occupied my evenings, and I was very seldom with my family, and they had not looked for my coming. My little daughter, much to my annoyance, was absent. When her mother told me she had permitted her to go to a neighbor's house for an hour, I was unreasonably angry, and sent for her, and declared that if she went there again, I would punish her.

"'Several weeks after this, I was again unexpectedly at home. Again, my little girl was away. My wife was much troubled in having to tell me that – being quite sure that I had no real objection to her going into our neighbor's house where she was under the very best influence, and not thinking I would be at home – she had allowed her to go. I sent for the little girl and chastised her. Just before going to her room, she came, and between sobs, said, "Papa, I am sorry I disobeyed you. I thought perhaps you would be willing if Mama was. And Mr. Smith prays with his children every night and I went in to pray for you, Papa." The next day my little girl was laid up with scarlet fever, and in three weeks I followed her little body to the grave. I came back to the house, I trust, a humbled, chastened man. My family altar was again erected, my place in the prayer meeting again filled. And by God's help, I purpose from now on to live for Him. But, my friends, my getting into the world, and what it has cost me, is a sad memory. May God lead you to accept His will without waiting for the discipline.'"

If every father in the church were right with God, it is absolutely certain that we should soon find the church throbbing with the mighty power of God.

CHAPTER SEVEN

A NEVER-FAILING PRINCIPLE

For the wages of sin is death, but the free
gift of God is eternal life in Christ Jesus
our Lord. (Romans 6:23)

There is no principle more unfailing than this. It is one of God's inevitable laws, and it is the more emphasized because it is stated by Paul the apostle, and is found in the epistle to the Romans.

The whole letter to the Romans is a masterful argument, and Paul himself was a mighty writer. No verse in Romans should properly be taken separately for treatment or studied out of its context. Paul is such a logician, and his epistle is such an argument, that it must be studied as a whole to be appreciated.

Each writer or speaker has words unique to his own vocabulary.

Peter's word is *precious*. He speaks of *precious*

promises, precious blood, and *a precious corner stone* or Savior.

Paul's words most frequently used are *for, but,* and *therefore.* The first two are to be found in the Scripture quoted above.

There are three *therefores* in the epistle to the Romans that should receive our special attention, and these three stand out like great mountain peaks in his argument.

Romans 5:1. *Therefore, having been justified by faith, we have peace with God through our Lord Jesus Christ.*

Romans 8:1-2. *Therefore there is now no condemnation for those who are in Christ Jesus. For the law of the Spirit of life in Christ Jesus has set you free from the law of sin and of death.*

Romans 12:1. *Therefore I urge you, brethren, by the mercies of God, to present your bodies a living and holy sacrifice, acceptable to God, which is your spiritual service of worship.*

In each case, we must study all that precedes if we would appreciate Paul's conclusions. In the first chapter of Romans, he is giving a striking description of sin. No better picture of the condition of the human heart has ever been drawn. It is said that when one of the missionaries was translating this Scripture into Chinese, his Chinese amanuensis refused to continue the work when the first chapter of Romans was finished because he said he did not want to be guilty of making known publicly the condition of his own people.

Following the picture of sin is the reference to Israel, and following this reference Christ is offered for our sins, and because of faith in Him we are justified. In the sixth chapter, Paul strikes a note of warning, calling attention to the license that some people might feel it possible to indulge in because of justification, and at the close of this chapter he uses the Scripture with which this chapter is introduced: *For the wages of sin is death.*

The difference is shown between wages on one side and a gift on the other side. Wages calling for untiring energy and almost ceaseless toiling, and gifts accepted with no effort put forth at all except the outreaching hand to receive the gift, present to us the difference between the two masters: one the Christian's Master, the other the one whom the world serves.

The background of Paul's picture here is sin. We cannot eliminate it from our consideration; if we do, other errors instantly creep into our thinking and ultimately into our living. Lax ideas of sin produce fruit in lax ideas concerning the necessity for an atonement. Sin is not simply an error, nor is it a mistake, but it is a damnable thing, too black to be described in human language. So great was it in the thought of God that it demanded an infinite sacrifice for which the blood of bulls and goats could no longer suffice. God

Sin is not simply an error, nor is it a mistake...

pity the man who, in the face of such a thought, trifles with sin, encourages its practice in his life, and seeks to cover it over in his heart. In the awful havoc that it has wreaked, it changes the expression of one's countenance.

The story of the two paintings by Leonardo da Vinci is one that may be paralleled every day in actual life. The great artist had painted the face of a lovely child and was so fascinated by the picture that he kept it constantly before his gaze in his studio. The sight of the beautiful child's face tranquilized his soul in sorrow or in anger. He resolved to paint a picture that would be its opposite. Long and patiently, he searched for a model, but could find no face bad enough to parallel in hideousness the angelic beauty of the young face in his studio. Many years afterwards, when he had given up the search, he looked upon the almost inhuman countenance of a criminal, lying in despair on the floor of a prison cell. At length he had found the model for whom he had been looking. He painted the terrible face, and then learned to his amazement that the crime-hardened man and the angel child were one and the same. Brutal passions had transformed the angel into a demon. The body had been refashioned by the mind.

Sin undermines character. I have never known of someone making a conspicuous public failure that investigation did not prove the fact that the one failing had begun with the commission of some almost trifling sin, and the one transgression made the next easier, until at last the wreck was complete.

In India, the white ants burrow their way into the rafters of the cottages. So small is their work that it is not noticed by the casual passerby; but when the storm comes, the house that seemed strong falls almost with the first touch of the wind, and the wreck is complete. The work began with the burrowing of an ant hole. So do men fail.

Sin breaks up households. I went one day to call upon a young businessman to ask him to come to Christ. I knew his heart was tender because of the recent death of his wife, but while he received me graciously, he declined to accept Christ, saying that he had no need of Him. He said

68

his character was strong and that he had every inclination against sin. But one day my telephone bell rang sharply, and I was called back into the same house to comfort four little children who were not only motherless but were also worse than fatherless. In a downtown hotel, the father was lying dead by his own hand. Shortly after our conversation, a strong temptation had overpowered him. He had changed one figure in his ledger books, and he died a debtor to the extent of a quarter of a million of dollars. His children were scattered almost literally to the four winds. Their names were changed so that they might forget their father, and he is in eternity awaiting judgment.

This is sin. It not only blights the offender himself, but it also injures others, and this is the sad thing about sin. James E. Talmage once said there were five acts in the tragedy of an alcoholic father, which he called "the rum tragedy."

Act One

A graduation scene where a young man gaining the honors of his class and the applause of the commencement audience steps forth into life with every prospect of winning a victory.

Act Two

The sound of marriage bells is heard and the whole sky seems bright with promise that the life thus nobly begun shall go on with increasing power and strength.

Act Three

A cloud has begun to appear in the sky and the man whose future was so bright is beginning to go down under the touch of sin.

Act Four

A woman is waiting in a poorly furnished room with a child crying at her knees. She is looking and listening for the return of one who now comes home with an unsteady step, but she waits in vain.

Act Five

Three graves are in a dark place: the grave of a child who died of neglect, the grave of a wife and mother who died of a broken heart, and the grave of a father and husband who sent himself into eternity and learns today that the wages of sin is death.

Sin is small in its beginning, so small indeed that men do not fear it. They think that they can begin when they choose and stop when they please, but they wake up one day to learn that they have been forging chains of habit and are bound hand and foot.

While seated in the office of a friend who was an official on the Southern Pacific Railroad, he asked me if I had seen the big trees in California. When I told him that I had simply seen them from the car window, he showed me a measuring line on which was printed his affidavit that he had made measurements, which were astonishing. The circumference of one tree was 105 feet and the diameter 35 feet, while the height was something enormous. He said to me, "These big trees are sermons in themselves. They are the oldest things we know, and they never die except when some outside force is brought to bear upon them. How large would you think," he said, "the seed of a big tree might be?" And I answered, "Judging from the size, I should say it might be as large as a pumpkin." He smiled and held out before me on a piece of paper the seeds of the great trees, and they were smaller than a mustard seed. So it is with sin. It begins with an evil imagination, an impure thought, and unholy ambition, but the end is death.

Sin is deceiving in its influence.

Sin is deceiving in its influence. This is true of some diseases. Traveling through New Mexico and Arizona recently, where very many people are the subjects of the dreaded disease of tuberculosis, I failed to find one who felt the danger of his position. The disease is said to be flattering, and the subject thinks that he is growing better, until suddenly he is face-to-face with eternity. How many men there are who will tell you that they can go just so far and stop! How few there are that expect ever to be lost!

I have read that the vampire bat in the West Indies fans its victim to sleep while it sucks away its lifeblood. This is sin, and its wages is death.

Sin is sure in its progress. For every man in Christ and out of Christ, the Scripture should be plainly written, *Be sure your sin will find you out* (Numbers 32:23) There is no escape from this; hide it as securely as you please, but one day there will be a resurrection. It will come at the time when you least expect it and also at the time when you can least afford to meet it. In the island of Ceylon, I have been told that there are more than forty serpents whose stings are deadly. There is one at least, which, if it should sting your hand or foot, you would be dead in a minute, and yet death is not more sure as the result of the serpent's sting than it is sure as a result of the practice of sin.

Sin is degrading in its influence. It can tear down the strongest character and blight and mar the happiest future. The story is told of a man in New York City whose position was all that man could desire. Under the stress of temptation, however, he began to fail. He went from bad to worse, moved from one house to another, each time his apartments growing smaller. He became cruel in his treatment of his wife and children, and one day as he returned, maddened by the power of strong drink, his little two-year-old child ran to meet him. When picking him up in his fury, he then threw him from him. The child struck the stone step, and they picked him up dead. This is sin, and the wages of sin is death.

Sin is the worst sort of bondage. That poor deluded man who shot Andrew H. Green, the father of Greater New York, gave the following explanation for his crime: "I used to be a good man," he said, "but I sold myself to the devil and he made me do what I have done. I could not help myself." The raving of this poor soul is a picture of many another man. If you doubt it yourself, try to break some habit and to free yourself from some sin and see how it will pursue you.

Sin is sure in its punishment and its wages are something terrific – not only the sleepless nights, the condemning conscience, the weakened character, the blighted future, and the lost reputation. These things in themselves are bad enough, but the future baffles description. No word of mine could paint it black enough. The wages of sin is death.

The question may be asked, "What is the greatest sin?" There may be a difference of opinion concerning this among men. Some men count drunkenness the greatest, others imagine impurity to be the chief of all sins, and still others suggest that it may be dishonesty. But the Word of God has declared that the greatest of all sins is the rejection of Jesus Christ. When men stand face-to-face with God in judgment, the question will be not concerning one's impurity, dishonesty, or drunkenness, but rather this: "What did you do with Jesus Christ?" And upon the answer to this question, man will stand or fall at the judgment bar.

What is the remedy that can be offered to meet this awful condition? There are two suggestions made: one is born on earth, the other is sent down from heaven. The first is the suggestion of man. We are told that if our environment is only changed, our condition will be so much the better. It will be an easy thing for us then to break away from the power of sin. This certainly is not true. If environment had such power, Adam and Eve never would have sinned, for they lived in Paradise; Judas never would have fallen, for he was so near to Jesus Christ that it was possible for him to touch Him, to see plainly the expression of His countenance, and almost to hear the beating of His heart, and yet he sold his Lord and sent his soul to hell.

We are told again that if character is only strengthened and conduct is rightly ordered, the result will be the breaking away of sin. In other words, we are commanded to do our best and God will look with favor upon us. But this cannot be true, for we are sinners, and our sin has been against God. Many of those whom Jesus Christ came to save have lost all power of will and have almost lost the desire to be good and true. He is a mighty Savior to all such. Their characters are ruined; they can do nothing of themselves. It is a good thing to suggest to each person who desires to save the sinner that if his method of salvation is to prove effective, he ought to try it upon those who are the lowest down and the most depraved. If it fails with them, it is of no use to others. Our gospel is for all such, the gift of God is eternal life, and if the poor depraved sinner has simply strength enough to reach forth his hand as he would put it out to take a cup of water, he may be saved.

The gift of God is eternal life.

God's remedy, which was decided upon in heaven, is described in the text. *The free gift of God is eternal life.* In the Scripture we are told that *Christ died for our sins* (1 Corinthians 15:3), and that settles the sin question judicially. God could not look with indifference upon the smallest transgression. In order that He might be just and the justifier of all them that believe, He *so loved the world, that He gave His only begotten Son, that whoever believes in Him shall not perish, but have eternal life* (John 3:16). Therefore, if we desire to be saved, let us accept the gift – eternal life, which is only another way of saying "the life of the eternal." This life is in us; by means of it we are able to overcome temptation. It is in us; because of it we can rejoice in trial.

When Commander Booth-Tucker was paying a tribute to his noble wife at the funeral service held in Carnegie Hall, New York, he said, "I was one day talking to a man in Chicago, asking him to come to Christ, when he said, 'If God had taken your beautiful wife and left you alone with your children, would you still believe in Him?' And," said the great Salvation Army officer, "if that man is in the audience today, I want to say to him that God has taken my beautiful wife and left me alone with my children, and He has never been nearer to me than now, and I have never loved Him more." This is really being a Christian, and the strength to rejoice under such trial is the gift of God.

He is in us, making it possible for us to live as we ought to live. If we could accustom ourselves to ordering our days by some particular statement of Scripture, we would be surprised to see how bright the day would be. Let the motto of one day be: *Bear one another's burdens* (Galatians 6:2), or the truth for another day be: *Regard one another as more important than yourselves* (Philippians 2:3). And he who practices the presence of God in such a way, and lives according to the teachings of Christ, will find the days of earth to be days of heaven and his character transfigured.

I would like to make an appeal to all who may read these words. Such an appeal might stir the emotions and stimulate the memory, perhaps bringing before them the vision of a mother or the sermon of the preacher of olden days, and as a result of which the reader might be saved. If you go to a rescue mission and ask the most depraved person to tell you what it is that has saved him from final destruction and despair, he will tell you, "My mother's prayer" or, "My father's hope" or, "My Sunday-school teacher's influence."

There came one day into the city of St. Louis a Christian woman from the country, and she asked one of the ministers to permit her to accompany him to the hospital, as she had not visited such an institution before. She carried on her arm a basket of honeysuckle, and she wanted to place a sprig upon each cot in the hospital ward. I am quite sure that the fragrance of the honeysuckle could stir many a sacred memory. One of my friends told me one day in New York that the odor of a honeysuckle always took her back to her childhood home in the South, and she never could think of it without weeping. Passing from cot to cot, the country woman placed the flowers wherever possible in the hands of the sufferers. She came to one cot where a screen had been placed around it. This was a new experience for her. She put the honeysuckle in the dying girl's hand and was just turning away when she saw the girl's lips moving.

Bending down she heard the girl whispering, "Mother, I smell the fragrance of the honeysuckle outside my window." When she looked at the girl a second time she cried out, "Margaret, my child, my child!" for it was the woman's own daughter who had wandered away and was dying because of her sin. It was the fragrance of the honeysuckle that aroused the girl and resulted not only in reunion with her mother, but also in the winning of her soul to Christ. I am afraid when I think of men delaying the acceptance of Jesus Christ and see them trifling with sin. I hope that I might bring to your memory a picture of His suffering and dying and the plea made to you by someone in other days.

Not long ago in California, I was told of the salmon fishermen who work at the mouth of the Columbia River. Hundreds of little fishing boats put out at sunset, each having two fishermen on board. They sail to the spot where they are to work, then set their nets as the tide is coming in, and boat and net drift upward with the tide. Then the tide turns and the boat drifts back again to the sea. When the morning breaks, it is seen that the boat is near the breakers.

I am afraid when I think of men delaying the acceptance of Jesus Christ.

The fishermen go as far as they can, then begin to draw in the nets, drifting all the time towards death. One fisherman is seen stopping. Something holds his net. It is full, evidently, and he delays a moment too long, attempting to draw it in at any cost. Before he can escape, the boat is drawn outward again towards the sea and the fisherman is lost, all because of the moment's delay. So, I lift my cry to every halting, hesitating man, telling him that *the wages of sin is death, but the free gift of God is eternal life.* I beg you therefore, reader, to take the gift.

CHAPTER EIGHT

A STARTLING STATEMENT

The evil man will not go unpunished.
(Proverbs 11:21)

There are very many passages of Scripture that
ought properly to be read in connection with this
text, as, for example, *Fools mock at sin* (Proverbs 14:9),
for only a fool would. It is better to trifle with the pesti-
lence and expose oneself to the plague than to discount
the blighting effects of sin.

And again, *The soul who sins will die* (Ezekiel 18:4).
From this clear statement of the Word of God, there
is no escape. Or again, *You have placed . . . our secret
sins in the light of Your presence* (Psalm 90:8). There is
really nothing hidden from His sight. We may conceal
our sinful thoughts, and sometimes even our evil practices may be hidden from men, but not from God. Or
again, *When sin is accomplished, it brings forth death*

(James 1:15). Here is the progress of sin indicated, from which law there has never been the slightest deviation. But one of the sharpest texts in all the Word of God, and one that men somehow in these days seem to ignore, is Paul's expression, *Do not be deceived, God is not mocked; for whatever a man sows, this he will also reap* (Galatians 6:7). And if we compare this reference in the New Testament to the text in the Old Testament, the harvest indeed seems to be sure: *The evil man will not go unpunished.*

There is a note of truth in all of these statements for both saint and sinner. Jeremiah 30:11 reads: *"'For I am with you,' declares the LORD, 'to save you; for I will destroy completely all the nations where I have scattered you, only I will not destroy you completely. But I will chasten you justly and will by no means leave you unpunished.'"* The old prophet is speaking to the people of Israel, and while he tells them that they are God's people, nevertheless they will not entirely go unpunished. For if they sow to the flesh, they must of the flesh reap corruption.

If they sow to the flesh, they must of the flesh reap corruption.

In Deuteronomy 5:9 we read: *You shall not worship them or serve them; for I, the LORD your God, am a jealous God, visiting the iniquity of the fathers on the children, and on the third and the fourth generations of those who hate Me.* It is a solemn fact that the sins of the fathers descend upon the children until the third and fourth generations. It is more solemn that so blighting is the effect of sin that the fourth generation is the last;

there is no fifth. Even though we are pardoned for sin, we will not entirely go unpunished.

Certainly, it is true if one rejects Jesus Christ that punishment for him is absolutely sure.

Not long ago in the city of Chicago the following appeared in the *Inter Ocean* newspaper as an editorial under the title of "The Preaching That Moves":

To those who look upon men as they are, it is simply astounding that so many preachers should act as if the hope of reward alone could be efficient to move average mankind to leave sin and follow after righteousness.

In every other relation of human life, every man is constantly confronted with the alternative: Do right and be content; do wrong and be punished.

The pressure of fear as well as the pressure of hope is continually upon him. He knows that he may conceal his wrongdoing from the eye of man; but he is always under the fear of discovery and punishment.

But he goes to church, and in nine cases out of ten, the preacher, while insisting that he can hide nothing from the eye of God, says nothing to arouse in him that fear of God which is the beginning of wisdom.

If he turns from religion to science, he finds science more positive of the certainty of punishment than of the certainty of reward. Science cannot, for example, assure him of a long life, even though he scrupulously obeys hygienic laws. But it can assure him of a speedy death if he wantonly violates those laws.

Precisely because the consequences of sin in punishment can be foretold more positively than the consequences of righteousness in reward is what makes fear the strongest influence dominating and directing human conduct.

Yet many preachers deliberately abandon the appeal to fear and then wonder why their preaching does not move men to active righteousness. When more preachers recover from the delusion into which so many of them have fallen, such complaints will diminish.

For all human experience proves that the preaching that appeals to fear of punishment as well as to hope of reward is the preaching that is really effective. This is the preaching of all the great preachers of the past and the present; it is the preaching that moves.

The statement of the text is exceedingly plain and the teaching is unquestioned. It is a good thing for us today to understand what sin is, for if we have a wrong conception of sin, it naturally follows that we shall have a wrong conception of the atonement. Without an understanding of sin there is no sense of guilt, and without the sense of guilt there is no cry for pardon.

The best definitions of sin that I have ever found are written in the Word of God.

I.

1. *Whosoever committeth sin transgresseth also the law; for sin is the transgression of the law* (1 John 3:4 KJV). The word *transgression* means to go across. Does your life parallel God's law or cross it? Your answer to this question determines the measure of your sin. You have only to read the Ten Commandments and try to mold your life by

them to find your answer. Better still, you have only to read these commandments in the light of Jesus' interpretation, where the look of lust is adultery, and anger without cause is murder, to see how far short you have come. And if this is true, then certainly you are a sinner, and the text is for you. *The evil man will not go unpunished.*

2. *All unrighteousness is sin, and there is a sin not leading to death* (1 John 5:17). Righteousness means right relations with God. You may make ever so strong a claim to right living and speak ever so vehemently concerning the good that you are accomplishing in the world, but the first question for you to settle is this: What is your relation to God and what have you to say about your acceptance or rejection of Jesus Christ? It is a solemn thought that whatever we do counts for nothing if our relation to God is wrong, while the little that we may do may count for much if we have taken the right position before Him.

3. *Therefore, to one who knows the right thing to do and does not do it, to him it is sin* (James 4:17). Omission according to this Scripture is sin; neglected opportunity is sin; shirking responsibility is sin; refusing to obey God is sin. And so when I ask you whether being a Christian is best and right and you acknowledge that it is, then if you are not a Christian this very fact is in itself sin, for when one knows the right and refuses to

do it, he is a sinner and the text is true: *The evil man will not go unpunished.*

4. *But he who doubts is condemned if he eats, because his eating is not from faith; and whatever is not from faith is sin* (Romans 14:23). Acted doubt is sin. If you have a doubt concerning the sinfulness of certain things, then to do those things is sin. If I have the least doubt concerning the amusements that may be questionable or the position that may be doubtful, so long as a doubt or a question remain, these things are sin, and the Bible states the fact that *the evil man will not go unpunished.*

5. *And He, when He comes, will convict the world concerning sin and righteousness and judgment* (John 16:8). Unbelief is the chief of sins. This is to reject Jesus Christ; it is to close in our own face the door of hope; it is to trample the blood of the Son of God under our feet, and it means also to insult the spirit of grace.

One morning in the city of New York, at about two o'clock, a man dashed down the street and, passing two men, rushed onto the pier. They could not tell how old he was nor how he was dressed, but they saw him strip off his overcoat and hat, and, before they could move to save him, he plunged off the end of the pier. There was a short rope lying nearby. Seizing it, the men ran to the point from which he had jumped. They threw the rope toward the struggling figure that they could just make out below them. The rope fell a foot and a half too short. Then they ran back to the gas station and got a longer rope. The ice was running so thick in the river that the man's head and shoulders were still to be seen above the water when they returned. Taking careful aim, they threw the rope squarely across the struggling form, shouting, "Catch it and we'll pull you in." The unknown man, however, making a last effort, threw the rope aside, and shouted back, "Oh, to h—— with it! I'm through!" Then he sank out of sight. That is a picture of the man who, having mercy and grace in Jesus Christ offered to him, spurns everything that God offers, and is therefore hopeless.

Sin separates us from God.
Sin separates us from each other.
Sin pollutes us and we become impure.
Sin deceives us and we are in danger and know it not.

A friend of mine walking along the streets of Cincinnati early one morning saw a young girl standing upon the very edge of the roof of one of the highest office buildings. She was carefully balancing herself and every moment it seemed as if she would fall. The elevator was not running. He made his way hurriedly to the roof of the building, walked carefully across it, seized her by the hand, and drew her back to find that she was sleepwalking, and all unconsciously she was standing on the very brink of eternity. This is what sin does for us, and it is a solemn thought that for all such, the text is true: *The evil man will not go unpunished.*

II.

I do not make my appeal, however, on the ground that the punishment is all for the future, for that is indeed sure. I ask you the question, "Do you believe in heaven as a place of rewards?" If so, the same argument will prove the existence of hell. "Do you reject hell because it seems to you to be inconceivable?" Then the same argument will blot heaven out of existence. What it is that awaits the wicked, I am sure I do not know, only that it is to be away from God, with the door of hope shut forever. The Bible tells me that there is weeping and wailing and gnashing of teeth, for the wicked shall not be unpunished. I lift my voice against the punishment here, for sin is so sure in its deadly work, it is so insidious in its influence, that before you know it, it is upon you. Just one day of trifling and you are gone.

Just one day of trifling and you are gone.

The people of Cheswick, Pennsylvania, will never forget the Harwick mine horror in 1904, when 181 dead men were taken from the mine. Under the direction of one of the mining engineers, a rescuing party started into the mine to see if there was any hope of saving the men who might yet be alive. The journey is described by one who volunteered to go with the engineer on his perilous journey.

When we got to the foot of the shaft, Mr. Taylor lighted a cigar. He blew out a great cloud of smoke and watched it drift into a passage. "This way," he said, "the smoke will follow the pure air draught." So we went on, Mr. Taylor blowing clouds of smoke, and we following them. Suddenly he wheeled and yelled, "The black damp[2] is coming!" The cigar smoke had stopped as though it had come to a stone wall and was now drifting over our heads. We ran with death at our heels, ran with our tongues dry and swelling and our eyes smarting like balls of fire. It seemed only a minute until Mr. Taylor shrieked and fell forward on his face. He crawled along for a while on his hands and knees, and then fell again and lay still. I stopped for a second, with the idea of carrying him.

Then I realized how hopeless that was. We were still a quarter of a mile from the foot of the pit. He was a very heavy man, and I, as you see, am small and weak. Again, I ran choking and beating my head with my hands. I fell, cut my face, called upon God, struggled to my feet, and fell again. So, I plunged on, falling and fighting forward. Black madness came upon me. The horrible, sickening poison gas from the mine was tearing my heart up through my dry throat. My brain was bursting through my temples. Then a stroke, as though by a sledgehammer, and I knew nothing more. They found me at ten minutes past one Tuesday morning. At first, they thought I was dead. Then they saw my head rise and fall while I weakly pounded on a rock with a stick that I had caught in my delirium.

This is to me a striking picture of what sin does for us. There is no one so strong but he may be overpowered by its awful influence. God save us from it, for *the evil man will not go unpunished.*

---

2   A poisonous gas

III.

Is there no hope? For it would seem from the message thus far as if nothing but despair was ahead of us. Two ways to escape from the power of sin have been suggested: one is man's way, the other is God's way. Let us consider them both.

1. Man's way. Man suggests reformation, but how about the sins of the past? They are still untouched. Man tells the sinner to do his best, but how about the will, which has been weakened by sinful practices and which seems unable to act? Man tells the depraved to change his surroundings, but how about the heart that is unclean? The fact is, man's way will not save us.

In January 1904, the American liner SS *New York* left Southampton and came into the New York harbor with a sad story to tell. A sailor was suspended over the side of the vessel making repairs when an enormous wave tore him away and he was very soon under the forefoot of the ship. The waves began to carry him away and a lifeline was thrown to him with a buoy attached.

The fact is, man's way will not save us.

The sailor, sometimes visible and then obscured by the rising of a swell, grasped the line and a cheer went up. He took a half-turn with the line around his waist, was rolling himself over into the knot of the line, and it looked as if he would be saved. The sailors on deck were just about to haul him in. The poor fellow's hands and fingers must have been numb with the cold, for he suddenly rolled out of the half-formed knot, losing his grip upon the line. None of the passengers could help the man, none of the crew dared jump to his rescue, and no boat could live in such a vortex. The sailor who was struggling and being whirled around and bobbing like a cork, his oilskins partially spreading out and sustaining him, kept drifting farther and farther away.

Aroused by the commotion, the second officer came on deck just as the sailor lost his hold. Tossing aside his cap, overcoat, and jacket, he told the seaman to tie a bowline hitch around his body and lower him away. The volunteer lifesaver was cheered by the passengers as he went over. It was bitter cold, the sleet sharp, and the swells ugly. A strong swim in the trough of the seas and over the crests and the officer might reach the seaman. It was his only chance.

He had no more than touched the ocean spray before the waves hurled him against the side of the steamer again and again, bruising his ankle and knee, but he struck out bravely and gradually drew nearer the sailor. For fifteen minutes, the senior second officer struggled. During one of his brave spurts in the direction of the struggling man, he looked up to the rail. The practiced eye of the seafaring man saw something that caused him suddenly to turn and fight his way back to the ship. The line was too short. The seaman holding the line attached to the officer had in his hands the mere end of it, and there was not another bit to pay out. It was a 120-yard line, "all gone," and the officer was only halfway to the drowning man. It was too late to splice another. Had it been thought of in time, the man might have been saved. A longer struggle was useless, and the officer allowed himself to be hauled aboard, leaving the helpless man to go to his last account. That is always the difficulty with man's effort to save the lost. It does not reach far enough and fails just at the time when it ought to hold.

2. God's way. *The blood of Jesus His Son cleanses us from all sin* (1 John 1:7). That is God's message. *Let the wicked forsake his way and the unrighteous man his thoughts; and let him return to the LORD, and He will have compassion on him, and to our God, for He will abundantly pardon* (Isaiah 55:7). This is God's invitation.

I, even I, am the one who wipes out your transgressions for My own sake, and I will not remember your sins (Isaiah 43:25). This is God's pledge, and He has never failed to keep it.

In the old days when England and Scotland were at war, the English came up against Robert the Bruce, King of Scots. They drove him from his castle and as he fled away from them, they let loose his own bloodhounds and set them upon his trail. His case seemed hopeless. He could hear the barking of the hounds in the distance and those who were with him had just about given up in despair. But not so with Bruce. He came to a stream flowing through the forest, he plunged in, waded three bowshots up the stream, and then came out upon the other side. The hounds came up to the stream, stopped, and sniffed. They had lost the track. They turned back defeated, and Bruce in time won the day. Is it not like this with our sins? Like a pack of hounds, they are after us, and wherever we flee they are close upon us. *The wages of sin is death,* I am told, but I have found the way of escape. Here flows a stream that runs red with the blood of Jesus Christ, and I plunge in and am free.

> There is a fountain filled with blood
> Drawn from Immanuel's veins;
> And sinners, plunged beneath that flood,
> Lose all their guilty stains.

CHAPTER NINE

A MESSAGE TO MEN ON THE GRACE OF GOD

I, even I, am the one who wipes out your transgressions for My own sake, and I will not remember your sins. (Isaiah 43:25)

Apart of this chapter I owe to another. In looking over an old volume of sermons preached by H. Grattan Guinness in 1859, I came across the message that he delivered with the above text as a basis. So deep was the impression made upon me by my first reading of the sermon that I have taken Mr. Guinness's outline and many of his suggestions and I call your attention to a great message to men.

He said, "If one should enter a jewelry store and ask to see a diamond or any other precious stone, the jeweler would first spread upon his showcase a black cloth and then place the diamonds upon it, not only for protection, but also in order that the black background might bring out distinctly the brilliancy and worth of the gems." So God gives His best of all His promises with the dark picture of sin clearly and thoughtfully portrayed. In Isaiah 43:22-24 we read: *Yet you have not called on Me, O Jacob; but you have become weary of Me, O Israel. You have not brought to Me the sheep of your burnt offerings, nor have you honored Me with your sacrifices. I have not burdened you with offerings, nor wearied you with incense. You have bought Me not sweet cane with money, nor have you filled Me with the fat of your sacrifices; rather you have burdened Me with your sins, you have wearied Me with your iniquities."*

And in these verses God says that His people have not called upon Him in prayer, they have not presented their offerings, nor have they presented themselves to Him. He also affirms that they have become weary of Him and that they have also wearied Him with their iniquities, and then He exclaims, *"I have not burdened you with offerings, nor wearied you with incense."* With these clear statements He gives us the gracious statement of the text: *"I, even I, am the one who wipes out your transgressions for My own sake, and I will not remember your sins."* Notice the division of the text as it regards sins:

First. They are blotted out from God's Book.

Second. They are blotted out with God's hand.

Third. They are blotted out for His sake.

Fourth. They are blotted out from His memory.

A more admirable outline of a text of Scripture I do not know; a more cheering message for a child of God I have never found.

I.

Not long ago in Chicago, a young man was induced to confess to the killing of his father and mother to someone whom he thought was his friend. As the confession was being made – as he supposed to only one person – it was all being taken down by those who were near enough to hear him speak, and when he appeared before the court, his own confession was used against him and sent him to a life imprisonment in the penitentiary. What was true of this young man is true of us. Every sermon the minister preaches is recorded, every word an individual speaks is put down. It is a solemn thought to realize that we shall give account at the judgment even for our idle words.

Science has proven that our acts, our words, and even our thoughts make their indelible record.

Not long ago in our home, we came across a long-unused phonograph. We started it going, placing upon it one of the cylinders that had been packed away with the phonograph, and were startled to hear the voice of someone who had been dead for years. We heard the message he dictated, the song in which he joined, and the laugh with which he closed it, and yet his voice had long been silent in death. There is not a sin of your youth that has not made its record; not a passion of your mature years that does not stand somewhere against you; not an act, a feeling, or an imagination that has not been indelibly written, no, not all the changes of time, and not all the efforts of man can wipe these things out.

In the British Museum there is a piece of stone, not larger than the average Bible, at least four thousand years old, and in the center of the stone there is a mark of a bird's foot; four thousand years ago, the track was made and for four thousand years the record has stood. If these things are true of us (and they are, according to the Word of God), then what prospect is there for us but that of eternal punishment? For when we stand at the judgment, there shall appear before us the sins of omission and the sins of commission, the sins we had forgotten and the sins we have but recently committed against ourselves, against our fellow man, and against God.

There is not a sin of your youth that has not made its record.

It is indeed a black picture, and with whitened faces and rapidly beating hearts we ask, Is there any hope? I bring you God's gracious answer to this important question: *"I, even I, am the one who wipes out your transgressions for My own sake, and I will not remember your sins."* Notice it is the voice of God speaking. *"I, even I,"* He exclaims, *"[will wipe] out your transgressions."* It is, first of all, a commercial term. We were in debt to God, hopelessly in debt, and our obligation was canceled; over against my sin is placed the righteousness of the Son of God, and I am free.

> Jesus paid it all,
>   All to Him I owe;
> Sin had left a crimson stain,
>   He washed it white as snow.

It is, second, a chemical expression, for it is a picture of God applying the blood of Jesus Christ to every page of the record written. The sins of our youth long ago passed out of mind, the sins of our manhood that have taken up every part of our being, and the sins of today – all have gone, for He Himself has blotted them out. When we realize that we are forgiven of God, it means more than if we were forgiven of men, for in the power of His forgiveness our past sins are gone, they shall not even be mentioned against us, and the fear of judgment is taken away, for Jesus Himself says, *"Truly, truly, I say to you, he who hears My word, and believes Him who sent Me, has eternal life, and does not come into judgment, but has passed out of death into life"* (John 5:24). It is the Passover story all over again: *When I see the blood I will pass over you* (Exodus 12:13). Thus our sins are blotted out.

II.

It is with God's hand that the work is done, and for very many reasons this is a great comfort to us.

First. Because it was God's hand that made the record. It was He who put down all your sins. He never rested in His work; week after week, month after month, year after year, the recording work was being done until your record became blacker than the blackest midnight. And behold, the hand that made the record blots it out.

Second. It was His hand against which you offended. Your sin was against yourself. It is true it hurt your character and lowered your self-respect, but more especially it was against God, for you despised His authority, forsook His service, broke His laws, defied His justice, grieved His Spirit, and crucified His Son. And behold, it is the hand against which you committed all these offenses that blotted out your transgressions.

Third. It is the offended hand that blots them out. It was the hand that opened the fountains of the deep, and behold the floods came, the waters above and the waters below clasped their hands, and destruction was everywhere except in the ark. It was His hand that brought destruction upon the cities and the plain, consuming them with a mighty flame, and it was His hand that opened the sea for the children of Israel and then closed the sea over the pursuing Egyptians. The very thought of the offended hand makes us tremble, but behold it is this hand that blots out all our transgressions.

Fourth. It is the hand of justice that does the work. The same hand wrote, *The evil man will not go unpunished* (Proverbs 11:21), and wrote again, *The soul who sins will die* (Ezekiel 18:4), and wrote again, *The wages of sin is death* (Romans 6:23). This hand is stretched forth on our behalf. I do not doubt the question has often come to us: How can God be just and the justifier of them that believe? (Romans 3:26 KJV). In the light of such statements as these just quoted, I am sure it is for this reason: It is for the offering of the just for the unjust. *He made Him who knew no sin to be sin on our behalf, so that we might become the righteousness of God in Him* (2 Corinthians 5:21). A man was needed for such an offering, and Christ became man. The man required must be born under the law, so Christ came in the likeness of sinful flesh. The man born under the law must be without sin, so He was born pure. The man born under the law and without sin must be willing to die, and so He came saying, *"I delight to do Your will, O my God"* (Psalm 40:8). And the man born under the law, without sin and willing to die, must be able to provide an atonement that would make the wandering sinner and the loving God one. So, Christ was offered to God and thus furnished a joint sacrifice of sufficient power and magnitude to save the whole world. It is this hand of God that blots out our transgressions.

> *A man was needed for such an offering, and Christ became man.*

Fifth. It is the hand of the Supreme Being that does the work. What a word of encouragement this is! It was this hand that made the worlds and hurled them off into space. It was this hand that created man and made him in the likeness of the image of God. It was this hand that formed the countless number of angels and has always directed their heavenly movements. It was this hand that wrote the word upon Sinai. And it is this hand that holds the kingdoms of heaven and hell. He blots out our transgressions. From His position there can be no appeal; with such a work as this, *who will bring a charge against God's elect?* (Romans 8:33). Would God who justifies do it, or Christ who died consent to it? In the light of such a thought the apostle Paul says, *For I am convinced that neither death, nor life, nor angels, nor principalities, nor things present, nor things to come, nor powers, nor height, nor depth, nor any other created thing, will be able to separate us from the love of God, which is in Christ Jesus our Lord* (Romans 8:38-39).

III.

Our sins are blotted out for His sake. God saves the sinner not alone because of pity for him, and certainly not alone because he is in danger of hell, but in order that He may glorify Himself. And this is no selfish glorification, but rather it is in order that He may show to us now and throughout all the ages what He really is. God has made different revelations of Himself. We have beheld His wisdom in creation, in His providence, and in His Word. We have seen His justice in that He gave His only begotten Son to die for poor lost men; we have seen His power in the working of miracles and in the transforming effect of His grace. It remains for us to see His love in the story of salvation, for until you behold Him as a Savior of the sinner, you do not know Him. It is this that shall make us not only rejoice here in time but also rejoice with joy unspeakable in eternity.

The apostle Paul writes in Ephesians 2:7-8, *So that in the ages to come He might show the surpassing riches of His grace in kindness toward us in Christ Jesus. For by grace you have been saved through faith; and that not of yourselves, it is the gift of God.*

IV.

Our sins are blotted out from God's memory. The last of this wonderful text is to me the best. When we detect a failure of memory here in this world among our friends, it is evidence of weakness, but it is no weakness in God to forget. I was listening not long ago to a distinguished lecturer, one of America's old heroes, when suddenly he paused, became greatly confused, and turned helplessly to his audience. The name of one of his great characters had passed

Our sins must have been a grief to Him.

from his memory and he could not recall it. I heard a gentleman sitting near me say, "This is the beginning of the end with the old general." And it was so, for in a few months he was dead.

This is but another one of those expressions descriptive of God in which human language is used to describe a great thought and in which human language is too poor an agency to convey all the depth of the meaning. It is just another picture of God stooping down to meet our weakness, and it is God assuring us that our sins are gone completely. It is as if they had never existed, for they shall never stand against us, and in the day of judgment they shall not even be mentioned. Our sins must have been

101

a grief to Him just as the sin of a child here is the cause of sorrow to an earthly parent; but they are not so any longer, for He has forgotten them. The Bible represents God as being angry because of our transgressions, but if ever there was anger with Him, it is not so any longer, for you cannot be angry with a person whose injury against you, you have entirely forgotten. We do not in this world speak of what we have forgotten, nor will God speak of our sins. We do not punish what we have forgotten, nor will God permit us to be punished, for He has blotted out our transgressions and will remember them no more. There is no awaiting penalty for your sin, there is no judgment to meet at the great white throne, and there is no hell for you at the last, for your sins for Christ's sake have been forgotten.

If you cast a stone into the water and it sinks away, there is for a time a ripple where the stone has gone down, but in a moment, it has gone forever and you can see it no more. So, God has cast our sins into the sea and the place where they have gone cannot even be found.

V.

But what must I do to take advantage of all this gracious offer of God? I answer according to the Scripture: There must be true repentance. Repentance is a change of mind; it is having a new mind for God. There must be regeneration. Regeneration is a change of nature; it is a new heart for God. There must be conversion. Conversion is a change of living and a new life for God. If we would be born from above, we must accept God's Word.

Two friends were conversing one evening. One of them with a skeptical mind had rejected the Bible because it did not tell him the things that he wanted to know. He insisted on knowing how the worlds were made and demanded that he should be told concerning the origin of heaven and why God permitted it, and because the Bible failed here, he would have none of it. Just as his friend was leaving the skeptic said to him, "Here is my lantern. I want you to take it and it will light your way home."

But the lantern was refused by the Christian man, for, he said, "This lantern will not light up the mountains in the distance, nor the valley stretching away at my feet."

His friend was amazed. "Man," he said, "take the lantern; it will make a road for you across the prairie step-by-step and light your pathway home."

"Oh," said the Christian man, "if that is true, then I will take it. But listen to me. So is the Bible, not so much for distant paths of investigation. It is not so much to tell us concerning creation and existence, although it does shed light there, though we will know these things perfectly in time. But it is for the path at your feet, and it will light you home a step at a time."

The skeptical man saw it in an instant. He took God's Word and came back again to the faith of his childhood.

So I offer it to you. With its promises as a sure foundation, with its commands carefully received and followed out, you too may pass from darkness to light, and you may claim from God this text of mine that says, *I, even I, am the one who wipes out your transgressions for My own sake, and I will not remember your sins.*

CHAPTER TEN

A CHURCH FOR MEN

To one acquainted with the Reverend S. B. Alderson, D.D., of Portsmouth, Ohio, and his work, it would almost seem as if the absence of men from the services of the church was largely the fault of the minister himself. For several years Dr. Alderson has been conducting, in connection with his church, a successful Sunday afternoon service for men. The attendance began with eight men present. It is now a very ordinary thing to see five or six hundred men in the audience every Sunday afternoon.

At my suggestion, Dr. Alderson writes concerning his work as follows:

"A few years ago, in a meeting for men, conducted by J. Wilbur Chapman, I received a precious blessing upon my own soul. There, I made up my mind that throughout the remainder of my ministry, be it long or short, I would devote more effort than in the past to that large, indifferent, and neglected population who had so much in this world to contend against. I would by God's grace and assistance try to save the men, a group of people who realize so little their eternal danger and in whom I had always found a hopeful element to work with when properly approached.

"My church at that time did not differ from the ordinary run of churches, having a small nucleus of devoted members and a majority attendance of females at its regular religious services. The problem now was how to reach the men with the gospel, for I had no advantages either in myself or in my congregation, except that of a humble, faithful pastor and preacher. The work was before me. How to inaugurate it and at the same time enlist the enthusiasm and cooperation of my own male church members, was the question to be decided.

The women had their literary and musical clubs, which brought them together frequently – which they greatly enjoyed, which they enthusiastically attended – but there was nothing of the kind that brought the men together in assemblies outside of their narrow denominational church services. The men met one another in their daily business relations, but in higher social and spiritual relations they were not really acquainted. Nothing ever threw them together in this capacity. Church and social circles had formed cliques and rings, which brought the same individuals into frequent contact with one another, but there was no wider tie of mutual interest that brought them together as a body, massed for the purpose of studying their moral and religious interest.

"Assuming that they would appreciate this higher movement on their behalf, I announced a meeting in the lecture room of my church to be held on Friday evenings, throughout the winter months. I then selected two or three live topics of local interest about which men were thinking, and started off to find a few well-known and thoughtful men in the community who would consent to open the discussion upon these several topics. On the first evening, it rained, and only eight men were present. In a few weeks, however, the interest extended to a wider circle of men, and we soon had an average attendance at the meeting of over two hundred men. These meetings were never organized. They had no name, no officers, no expenses, no constitution nor bylaws; there was only a committee of three men selected to provide topics and assign them to qualified speakers.

The subject of religion was never once introduced, neither by song, nor by prayer. The object was to bring men together as nearly as possible upon an equal degree of freedom, and that no man should have his convictions or prejudices wounded, no matter what might be his denominational or political opinions. The discussions were open to all alike. Even the pastor did not assume any privileges or intrusion above the others. He was the most quiet and modest man in the company. He went there not to tell others what *he* knew, but to gather from the experience and thought of the others all that they had learned, and he hereby acknowledges that he gained much practical information of men and their ways, which has since been of excellent value. The pastor's supreme effort was to bring these men together socially, to help them to know each other, to draw them toward himself, and to win their esteem and affection, so that he might be useful to them in the future. It required a good deal of tact not to offend their prejudices nor to antagonize their opinions, and to hide from view his own ultimate motive, but it won in the end.

"Perhaps an explanation of the nature of the topics selected and discussed at these meetings would be interesting. The aim was to make everything intensely helpful and instructive to young men who, because of their daily employment, did not have time either to read or attend school. The point was to get the older and experienced and successful ones to tell for the benefit of others what they had learned. Some of the topics as I remember them were these: 'An Easy and Practical Lesson in Arithmetic,' by the principal of the business college; 'Banking, The Deposit, Circulation, and Protection of Money,' by a banker; 'Wages, How to Invest Small Savings,' by a manufacturer; 'Building and Loan Associations, How They are Managed, and What Advantages They Offer to Small Investors,' by the president of one of these associations; 'How to Make Farming Pay,' by a farmer; 'The Personal Care of the Human Body,' by a physician; 'The Sanitary Care of the Home,' by a physician; and 'Legal Forms for Drawing Up Notes, Bills, Contracts, and Mortgages,' illustrated on the blackboard by an attorney. To my personal knowledge, many men derived valuable financial, commercial, and physical benefit from the discussion of these and related themes.

"These meetings continued through two winters, with unabated interest. No one derived more good from them than did I, the writer. I learned to know men – their habits of thought, their peculiar inclinations, what interested them, what would attract them, what good thing remained in them underneath all their roughness, how to love them and talk to them, how to win their confidence and admiration, and how to point them to that Savior in whom I now know that the heart of the degenerate, the drunkard, the saloonkeeper, and the gambler longs to find and rest upon in peace.

"Before the second winter closed, an additional 'Men's Meeting' was appointed for Sabbath afternoons, to be of a gospel character and led by one of their own number – some man of approved Christian standing. An invitation was extended to all male persons over sixteen years of age, and at the same time a promise was given that these meetings would be undenominational. They would not be in the interest of the congregation whose church building was occupied, but the sole purpose would be to encourage the religious life in men – to bring them to see their need of Christ as the Savior of sinners, as the safe and only reliable shelter against their manifold temptations. Then, after they were converted, the plan was to send them to unite with the church of their choice, whether Protestant or Catholic. Men will act with more freedom in the presence of men than in a mixed audience, thus the rule barring boys was kindly enforced.

> *Men will act with more freedom in the presence of men than in a mixed audience.*

"The promise, never to ask any man converted in these meetings to unite with our church nor to use these meetings in any way to my personal advantage, has been strictly adhered to both by myself and my coworkers, until the whole community has learned to confide in our integrity and to admire our unselfishness. They believe that we are honest and have the glory of God and the welfare of men truly at heart. It took the people some time to find this out, but the number of men who have gone into the other churches, when some of them preferred my church, has disarmed prejudice and suspicion completely. Whenever these men have talked with me, I have insisted that they accept Christ first of all, and after that I have advised them to anchor in the church where their families or their unique inclinations and ties might lead them.

Divisions in the home have been carefully guarded against. And let me say, that this broad, honest Christian method, closely followed, has commended itself to sensible men everywhere, both in the church and outside of the church, and has proven to be one of the most powerful factors in this work. This method has allayed the fear of pastors and invited the cooperation of all good people. The motive is high, unobjectionable, and cannot be disputed. Sectarianism, denominationalism, and ecclesiastical rivalry men dislike and hold themselves aloof from, until they become converted; after that they become wiser and more charitable toward what seems to be the necessary condition of the church upon earth.

"Now as to the meetings, I will address how to

arrange and conduct them. A successful meeting of any kind must be planned and provided for in advance. The first thing necessary is a cordial greeting to every man who attends. Let him meet this atmosphere of welcome on the threshold as he enters the building. Show him that the meeting has a smile and an extended hand for him. Have a committee of genial and popular men at the door to receive the first person who enters. As for myself, I never fail, as the pastor of the church, to shake hands and speak a kind word to every man before he leaves the room.

"Then be careful not to make any distinctions between men – not to show any preference or partiality in the manner of your greeting. Let everyone – the well-dressed or the poorly clad, the man of wealth or the man of poverty, the man who stands high or the man who is rated low, everyone – receive the glad hand. Ponder and act upon the words of the apostle James:

> *My brethren, do not hold your faith in our*
> *glorious Lord Jesus Christ with an attitude*
> *of personal favoritism. For if a man comes*
> *into your assembly with a gold ring and*
> *dressed in fine clothes, and there also comes*
> *in a poor man in dirty clothes, and you pay*
> *special attention to the one who is wearing*
> *the fine clothes, and say, "You sit here in a*
> *good place," and you say to the poor man,*
> *"You stand over there, or sit down by my*
> *footstool," have you not made distinctions*
> *among yourselves, and become judges with*

evil motives? Listen, my beloved brethren: did not God choose the poor of this world to be rich in faith and heirs of the kingdom which He promised to those who love Him? But you have dishonored the poor man. Is it not the rich who oppress you and per- sonally drag you into court? Do they not blaspheme the fair name by which you have been called? If, however, you are fulfilling the royal law according to the Scripture, "YOU SHALL LOVE YOUR NEIGHBOR AS YOURSELF," you are doing well. But if you show partiality, you are committing sin and are convicted by the law as transgressors. (James 2:1-9)

"Study this last verse carefully. Many of us have sinned in this respect. Our transgressions have turned the face of God away from our effort. So many ministers and church workers select from the community the men whom they want saved because these men are their relatives and a selfish desire will be gratified; because these men will give standing to the church of which they are members; because their change of life will increase the pastor's renown; or because their offerings will strengthen the church's financial situ- ation and make the salaries secure. Are these proper motives for any gospel worker? How they weaken the attack upon a sinner's security when no higher motive

Our transgressions have turned the face of God away from our effort.

than this prevails in the mind. Successful work must be unselfish and altogether for God's glory.

"My experience is that if a minister values men by the worth of their souls, and sees in every man whom he meets, irrespective of clothes, habits, or standing, the same value, and his supreme aim is to *save [a] soul from death* (James 5:20), then God will look upon his ministry with favor and he will have his reward from heaven. This may not be a popular idea to enforce in some churches, but it is scriptural and right. In all of my ministry, and especially in revival services, I have endeavored to impress my church people with this idea and have insisted that they should not pick out the men of their own choosing for the honors of salvation, but take them in the order in which Providence sends them.

Talk to them just as you happen to meet them, for God is directing in this matter as in all things, and it is our duty to seize His opportunities, not waiting for those of our own making. There was never an outpouring of any great power in any of the churches served by myself, except when first the people became as willing to save a drunkard as a moral man, as happy to save a gambler as an honest man, and as anxious to save a saloonkeeper as the most respectable man in the community.

"God taught me this lesson years ago in a most striking way. I was pastor of a church at Washington Court House, Ohio. For five weeks I preached to a faithful few in the lecture room. The situation seemed to be getting more desperate rather than more encouraging. My heart was breaking under what seemed to be an approaching failure. We needed more of the substantial, influential, well-to-do people of the town to counteract certain influences that were at work and to give the church a higher standing. We had our eyes on the families whom we wanted to reach, but we were not reaching them. They stood off as usual, mocking at our calamity. One morning a number of men promised that they would go out that day and talk religion to any and every man whom they met, that they would invite these individuals to the revival services, no matter how hard and wretched and wicked they had become. Many that day were startled by the first religious conversation of their lives. This was kept up for several days, and it is needless to say that *the wedding was furnished with guests* (Matthew 22:10 KJV).

Soon the town was on fire with interest. The main audience room of the church became crowded, the folding doors were opened to accommodate the increasing numbers, and still many were turned away. Many notable conversions occurred. We reached the people whom we at first wanted by beginning with the lowest strata of the population and working upward. In the following four weeks, 140 people were received. The meetings closed on a high tide because the pastor had become physically exhausted. The character of the work was quiet, deep, and permanent. The memory of it remains like a sweet fragrance with those people still. Thus, God taught us not to be *flattering people for the sake of gaining an advantage* (Jude v. 16), and I have tried ever since then to keep that lesson in mind.

"Next, have a singing book for every man. In this

day of inexpensive songbooks, there is no excuse for a church to not put a book into the hand of every man in the meeting. Have a male organist and a male leader of the singing. This is not the place for a choir nor for fine singing. Men hear enough of that in the usual church service. Have the men do their own singing. Let them read the words of the hymns and hear their own voices. Nothing in the world is finer or more inspiring than the voices of hundreds of men singing praises unto God. Give the singing a large place in the meeting.

"The pastor should not lead the meeting himself unless special existing conditions make it expedient that once in awhile he should preside. Of that he must be the judge. His opportunities to speak are numerous; let the men have the floor if you are going to have a men's meeting. The great point is to get others to work, to bring them prominently forward so that they will become committed to the movement. Do not lose sight of this aim. Show your tact in getting others to take hold. Your leader may be timid, but assure him that you will stand right by him and that he cannot fail. Sit near him, so that he will feel the strength of your presence, and if you see signs of his becoming embarrassed, be ready in an instant to come to his rescue before he realizes that he is breaking down.

"Do not allow any long silences or pauses to occur. Speak to a dozen men in advance and get them to promise that they will get on their feet, either to pray or to give testimony whenever they notice that a break occurs. It is a great thing to train your church members to take a voluntary part in your midweek prayer-meeting services. As a rule, I never call upon anyone either to speak or to pray in my Wednesday-evening service. We doubtless kill many prayer meetings by doing so. We call upon those who can speak to edification as a rule to take part. Consequently, often when they respond, they do so simply because they are ashamed to decline, when perhaps the spirit of devotion is absolutely foreign to their hearts at the time. In that case, the whole performance is a mockery.

Throw the meeting open! Give God's people liberty! Let the Spirit select the individuals whom He desires to use and speak through. And if you find the Spirit is not there to respond voluntarily, close your prayer meeting earlier, then go home after a good but short service rather than have a long but very formal one. What you want is prayer, much of it and from many lips. It will require training to develop your people in this direction, but when they are developed, then you can use them everywhere.

In the meetings for men, keep things going.

"In the meetings for men, keep things going. With a wise pastor on one hand and a good leader of the singing on the other, together with a ready organist, the meeting should move right along. I have yet to see the first man, however timid, fail and break down as a leader, but I have seen God use the feeble efforts of these men wonderfully in impressing others. They may not be able to occupy more than eight or ten minutes in remarks, but that is all right. What they do say comes from the heart and their trembling tones give great weight to their messages.

"Another point gained in having as many different men lead as possible is this: then the meeting is advertised each week under the name of a new leader and this gives variety. Besides, each leader has his special friends who will come out of curiosity to see and to hear him. Usually, the leader will become so deeply interested in his own meeting and so anxious to have it surpass the others in attendance, that he will spend a great deal of time personally inviting men. He will print cards containing his name and topic and will disseminate these through the shops and factories. The matter is on his mind all the while. You have no idea how anxious men are to hear from the Christian man who lives next door, who works in the same shop, who endures the same trials and temptations; how anxious they are to hear these men tell about the power of religion to make them strong and happy. They do not discuss these subjects as private individuals. Everything else is talked about, but not this. These meetings are a revelation.

"Be sure that your leader is a person of reputable Christian character and that he has been a member of the church long enough to convince others of his sincerity. Take him right into your pulpit with you and let him see that your desk is not simply a place reserved for an ordained man, but that it is the place for any man whose object is to save souls. Let him see that your pulpit is not a place for proclaiming altogether profound theological doctrines, nor for getting off fine essays, but that it is consecrated to God for saving men. If his heart is yearning for his fellow man, he can stand in it without the least embarrassment. In so doing, you bring yourself as a minister down to the level of your fellows. They begin to look upon you as their equal and their friend. They will love and admire you, and your opportunity over them will become wonderfully increased.

"Often, men are heard to remark that they can hardly wait from one Sabbath to the next, so excited are they for these meetings to come. And the evidence of this soul longing is seen in the fact of their coming by hundreds from all directions and gathering at the doors of the church, often fifteen minutes before the doors are open or before the ringing of the first bell, which is three-quarters of an hour before the time announced for the meeting to begin. Some of the notable effects of these meetings may be summarized as follows:

"First is the effect on my own church, which has a large number of male members on its roll and in its Sunday congregations, and then upon our Sabbath school, where the attendance of males never fails to outnumber the attendance of females. This is unusual and exceptional. There are from seventy-five to one hundred men in our Sabbath school every Sabbath morning.

"Secondly is the effect on the number of men who have received salvation in these meetings and made their first start, either by rising or by coming forward for prayer. I say it with due deliberation and with many evidences to confirm the statement, that it is my sincere belief that on average there has been a man converted and turned to God in every men's meeting that we have held. The presence of the Spirit is very marked.

Let those take courage from this to begin the work and see what God will do for them.

"Thirdly is the effect on the unusual number of reformed men in this city, now observed and often spoken of by those who have resided here for a long time and who knew how these men lived in their former days. Now their faces are bright; their bodies have the glow of health since the liquor has gotten out of them; their language is pure and clean; their habits are good; their clothes have improved in quality; their families are happy; their places in the sanctuary are filled; many of them will lead in public prayer; and their influence for good is unbounded. Where they have been without employment, we have made strenuous efforts to find something for them to do.

"Fourthly, other churches in the city, seeing the advantage of these meetings and deriving great benefit from them in the way of male additions to their membership, have followed the example of the Second Presbyterian Church. Often our largest attendance has been on the very Sabbath afternoons when there were three or four other men's meetings announced for the same hour.

"The deepest and most genuine revivals in my whole experience have uniformly commenced with the men. Has not God promised that it should be so? *Thus says the Lord GOD, "This also I will let the house of Israel ask Me to do for them: I will increase their men like a flock. Like the flock for sacrifices, like the flock at Jerusalem during her appointed feasts, so will the waste cities be filled with flocks of men. Then they will know that I am the LORD"* (Ezekiel 36:37-38).

"Recently in the men's meeting, conducted in this church in the presence of hundreds of men, the following thrilling incident occurred that brought tears to every eye and left its impression upon every memory.

"Two men entered the room together. One was somewhat in his fifties, the gray predominating in the color of his hair. His mouth was covered with a heavy, gray mustache. The other was a youth of about twenty-two with a smooth, bright, intellectual face. They were strangers to most of the men. They occupied adjoining chairs. When the meeting was about half through, the older man of the two arose with his arms folded across his chest and evident emotion in the tone of his voice and said, 'I heard that a man who for many years had been a great drunkard was going to lead this meeting. That is my trouble. If God can save him, will He not save me? Men, pray for me.' And with that he took his seat, overcome by his feelings.

"The young man at his side bowed his head in a lengthy silence, occasionally wiping away his tears with his thumb. After he had gotten somewhat composed, he arose and said, 'This man by my side who just asked for your prayers is my father. I do not know what brought him to this meeting. He has been for many years a hater of churches and Christian people. He has been such a wicked man and such an unkind husband and father. For many years I have been ashamed to bear his name, ashamed for people to know that I was his child. I am myself a Christian – a student in the seminary, studying theology – and hope someday to preach the gospel. I had given up on my father, believing him to be beyond redemption. I doubted whether God could save him. This is the happiest moment of my life. I shall never cease to thank God that I came to this meeting. I shall go back to my school with the happiest heart that ever beat in the bosom of a man.

Oh men, help me and do not forget him nor let him go. I must leave him with you. Let us pray.' Then dropping upon his knees, oh, what a prayer that boy uttered for his father! I weep as I write about it. That man is now a Christian and a church member. His wife told me this morning, 'I never hear the bell for your men's meeting that I do not thank God for what your church is doing for the men of this city.' His little daughter, six years old, sitting upon the floor, sewing doll rags, overhearing our conversation, looked up into her mother's face and said, 'I remember when Papa got his gun and drove us away from home.'"

CHAPTER ELEVEN

DR. MUNHALL'S MESSAGE

The following sermon is by L. W. Munhall, M.A., D.D. (evangelist), Philadelphia. It is much abridged, and the illustrations, which are quite numerous, are all omitted. It has always been delivered to audiences composed wholly of men – mostly young men. It was first delivered in 1872. It has been delivered 269 times, never twice exactly alike, but always following the same outlines and treatment. His audiences ranged from 150 to 8,600 people, with an average of nearly 1,800. The sermon has never been given without conversions being immediately secured, ranging from 7 to 529, and averaging considerably more than 100 per service, or an aggregate of about 30,000 souls. The time taken in its delivery has never been less than an hour.

"Rejoice, young man, during your child-hood, and let your heart be pleasant during the days of young manhood. And

*follow the impulses of your heart and the
desires of your eyes. Yet know that God will
bring you to judgment for all these things.*
(Ecclesiastes 11:9)

"Man is a free moral agent. He can do right or wrong, he can go to heaven or hell, as he pleases. If his mind is fully set to do wrong, God will not coerce him into doing that which is right. If he is determined to go to hell, God will not compel him to go to heaven. God always respects man's deliberate choice. As He said to His ancient people, '*I have set before you life and death, the bless-ing and the curse. So choose life in order that you may live*' (Deuteronomy 30:19), and just so does He leave the welfare and destiny of all men in their own keeping. In view of the tremendous issues of life, our responsibility, gentlemen, becomes as weighty as eternity.

*He still reminds us
that He is sovereign
and judge.*

"While God tells us, in effect, to do as we please, He still reminds us that He is sovereign and judge, and that we are accountable beings, and must, therefore, answer to Him for all we say and do in this life. Make your own choice, gentlemen, but do not forget that there is judgment here and hereafter for it all. If you always have this relentless fact in mind, no doubt you will always choose the right and the good. Such is the teaching of my text.

"What are the ways of your heart?

1. "Some one of you may have set his heart on getting

rich. If you mean to get your money honestly and use it wisely, it is a proper and laudable ambition, and I hope you may get $100 million. But, if you propose to get your money by dishonest and rascally methods, I hope you may spend your days in the poorhouse instead. You see, I am your friend and well-wisher; for money dishonestly gotten will always prove a curse to the man who gets it thus, and to his children after him. In these days of intense commercial activity, and a mad rush for wealth, with the almost innumerable grab-bag, get-rich-quick schemes that are constantly making seductive appeals to the young man ambitious to be rich, one needs to be cautious and careful, or he will soon find himself violating the Golden Rule. But if you have resolved to be rich even if it is at the expense of honor and conscience, go ahead and do as you please. God will not compel you to do otherwise, but there will be judgment for you, here and hereafter. Never forget it.

2. "Some one of you may have set his heart on having what he calls a good time. It is a weird notion some men have of what is a good time. I have known a young man to riot around town all night, full of whiskey and the devil, squandering his hard-earned money, ruining his physical and intellectual health, his reputation and character, breaking his mother's heart, and getting his head broken and pretty generally done for, and call that having a good time. You are at liberty to pursue such a course, and if you have settled upon it, God will not

interfere. But there will be judgment for you here and hereafter. Never forget it.

"What is the sight of your eyes? God's Word says, *Do not look on the wine when it is red, when it sparkles in the cup, when it goes down smoothly; at the last it bites like a serpent and stings like a viper* (Proverbs 23:31-32).

"One cannot buy a glass of honestly distilled whiskey in the United States. When I was a boy, the man who kept the country store usually kept a little brown jug under his counter, in which he kept what he called "O be joyful." He distilled it himself from rye and corn. If a man purchased more than a dollar's worth of goods, he was invited to take a drink. If he took more than he could tolerate, it made him foolish and silly. But men in their hurry to be rich found they could make whiskey easier and cheaper by the aid of drugs.

If a man gets more of the whiskey they now make than he can tolerate, he becomes a fiend incarnate and wants to kill somebody. This is the explanation for the alarming increase of crime in the country: It is the poison in the whiskey. There never was a case of hog cholera in the country until they began using drugs in whiskey making. The poison gets into the mash, it is fed to the hogs, and they get the cholera. If you, gentlemen, think you can put into your stomachs with safety to yourselves that which will give the cholera to hogs, of course you are at liberty to do so, but if you do, I think you are not very bright or wise.

"But the people are more largely given to beer drinking. I also believe you cannot buy one glass of honestly made, malty, hop-brewed beer in the United States. Here are sufficient reasons for thinking so: First, there are not enough hops raised in the United States to make the beer that is drunk in New York City alone. We are exporting almost as many hops as we are importing them. Second, from indisputable evidence in my possession, I know that while the output of beer is rapidly increasing, the use of malt is quite as rapidly decreasing. Third, the brewer, the jobber, and the saloonkeeper all get rich fast, and the beer is sold at a nickel a schooner. I know as well as I can know anything that not one man can get rich selling beer at that price, if it is made out of hops and malt, honestly. No, what is called lager beer is nothing but slop. Now then, gentlemen, if you wish to make slop pails of your stomachs, you are at liberty to do so. But in view of the fact that the stomach is the workshop of the body, and the center of the nervous system, I submit that it will be to your advantage not to misuse it after this fashion.

"It is said that about one hundred thousand persons die from alcohol every year in the United States. If this is approximately true, what a blighting and withering curse it is! Surely *it bites like a serpent and stings like a viper.* But I am inclined to think that far more than this great number fall victims to this damnable and damning traffic. There are two distinctive temperaments among men: the fierce and the lymphatic. Alcohol never digests or assimilates. No matter in what form it is taken into the stomach, it passes through the digestive fluids into the blood.

In the case of the man of the fierce temperament, it goes to his head, and becoming thereby top-heavy, he reels when he tries to walk, and clucks like an old hen when he attempts to talk. When this man dies, it is known of what he died, because he could not conceal it. But in the case of the man of a lymphatic temperament, it is otherwise. When the alcohol gets into his blood, it goes to the liver. He's the man of whom it is said, 'He carries his whiskey.' This is so because the liver is 'midship,' as sailors say. He can drink all day and walk a chalk line home. But he drops off suddenly, and they say it was heart-failure or apoplexy. Most of the people who know him believe this, because they never saw him drinking or drunk. But if you will cut him open and uncover his liver, it will appear like the bottom of an ironmonger's shoe; he has died of what the physicians call 'hobnail liver' – alcohol on the liver. Now then, gentlemen, you can squander your money for drink, disgrace yourselves, superinduce premature physical and mental decay, and go down to an untimely and dishonored grave and to a drunkard's hell if you so wish it; but surely such a course is unwise and wicked. Remember there will be a judgment here and hereafter. Never forget it.

Remember there will be a judgment here and hereafter.

3. "Job said, *I made a covenant with mine eyes; . . . For it is a fire that consumeth to destruction, and would root out all mine increase* (Job 31:1, 12 KJV).

"The eye is the doorway to the seat of the passions. If, like Job, we vow not to look upon anything that suggests an unclean or evil thought, our lives and minds will be pure and beautiful. If we give license to our eyes, then our thoughts and lives will be impure, vulgar, and lewd. For, if our passions are aroused, they are easily enticed by Satan into sin. Licentiousness is *a fire that consumeth to destruction.* I knew a young man who, when he reached his adulthood, had $50,000 in the bank subject to his check, and real estate worth much more. He did not 'make a covenant with his eyes.' His passions were aroused, and he went to the house of her whose *steps take hold on hell* (Proverbs 5:5 KJV). In less than five years his money and property were gone, and he was a physical wreck.

"I knew another young man who did not 'make a covenant with his eyes.' He was led into secret sin. He was an alumnus of a prominent university. He had begun the practice of law. One day in his office he put a pistol to his head and fired. The bullet did not penetrate his head but circled it under the scalp. He told the physician who was summoned of his sinful practices and said, 'They have become so loathsome to me that I do not want to live any longer.' This is the story of one-half of the suicides committed, as it is likewise an explanation for three-fourths of the idiocy and imbecility in the world today. It truly is *a fire that consumeth to destruction.*

"But not only this, it also *would root out all mine increase.* God's law declares that He visits *the iniquity of the fathers on the children, and on the third and the fourth generations of those who hate Me* (Deuteronomy 5:9). This is physiologically demonstrable. The descendants of a man who has indulged in licentious practices deteriorate until the 'third or fourth generations,' which will be found to be sterile. There will be no fifth generation for such a man. This is the story of the nations of antiquity. Brush back the dust of centuries and read. When they were virtuous, they increased in numbers, in strength, and in possessions. When they became great, they became sensual and then began to decline in physical and mental energy, until they reached a point where they were unable to successfully resist the encroachments and onslaughts of their ruder and more virtuous neighbors, and they ceased to be. Gentlemen, you had far better trifle with a wire with fifty-thousand volts upon it, than to fall into licentious practices. *It is a fire that consumeth to destruction, and would root out all mine increase.* But you are at liberty to do as you please. You can drop the reins on the neck of your lust and ride like Jehu toward hell. God will not compel you to be virtuous, but if you are so unwise, remember, there will be judgment here and hereafter. Never forget it.

"Let us now turn this around and consider the matter under discussion from another point of view.

"*First.* You are ambitious to be rich. You remember that I wished you well if you intended to get your money honestly and use it wisely. But do not forget there are some things worth infinitely more than all sordid wealth; do not barter these for gold. For instance, *Better is the little of the righteous than the abundance of many wicked* (Psalm 37:16). *A blameless conscience both before God and before men* (Acts 24:16) is of priceless value. Be able to look Godward and know you are obeying His holy laws, and look any man in the face and be able to truthfully say, 'I have done by you as I would be done by.' This is worth more to a man than all earthly possessions.

"Again, *A good name is to be more desired than great wealth, favor is better than silver and gold* (Proverbs 22:1). When my father died, he left me not a penny nor a foot of land, but he left me that which has been worth more to me than all money and property: the heritage of a clean, manly, and honorable Christian name and life. I have never seen the time nor place I was ashamed to acknowledge that David Munhall was my father. Be careful of your good name. It is of priceless worth.

"Also, Jesus said, *'Store up for yourselves treasures in heaven'* (Matthew 6:20). My brother, if you live to be eighty years old and then die, you will have lived only 29,220 days, or 701,280 hours. So, the longest life is very brief. I submit, gentlemen, that it is in every way better to live these days of our earthly sojourn in poverty, with a conscience void of offense toward God and toward men, preserving unsullied our good name, and then for all eternity enjoy the inexhaustible riches and unfading glories of the heavenly life, than at the sacrifice of conscience and a good name become a millionaire many times over, and then be banished from the presence of the Holy One into outer darkness where *there will be weeping and gnashing of teeth* (Luke 13:28).

"*Second.* Mere earthly pleasures are necessarily unsatisfying. They may, for the time, seem to satisfy, but too often, alas! indulgence in them is followed by regret and heartache. But when a man is reconciled to God, and has His presence to go with him and His unfailing blessing to rest upon him, then he can understand what the psalmist meant when he said, *How precious is Your lovingkindness, O God! And the children of men take refuge in the shadow of Your wings. They drink their fill of the abundance of Your house; and You give them to drink of the river of Your delights* (Psalm 36:7-8). As the rivers pour their floods ceaselessly into the sea, so the pleasures God will give to the obedient soul shall be all satisfying and constant. *It is the blessing of the LORD that makes rich, and He adds no sorrow to it* (Proverbs 10:22). In the end, earthly pleasures can have nothing to offer us that we desire or need. But to those who love and obey God, there are the all-satisfying pleasures here. And concerning the other life, we know that *in [God's] presence is fullness of joy; in [His] right hand there are pleasures forever* (Psalm 16:11).

"Third. The psalmist prayed, *Open my eyes, that I may behold wonderful things from Your law* (Psalm 119:18). The apostle Paul gave expression to the same thought when he prayed *that the God of our Lord Jesus Christ, the Father of glory, may give to you a spirit of wisdom and of revelation in the knowledge of Him. I pray that the eyes of your heart may be enlightened, so that you will know what is the hope of His calling, what are the riches of the glory of His inheritance in the saints* (Ephesians 1:17-18).

"Our sins have separated and estranged us from God.

God has *made peace through the blood of His cross,* by Him *to reconcile all things to Himself* (Colossians 1:20). But our *repentance toward God and faith in our Lord Jesus Christ* (Acts 20:21) are reckoned as certain elements in the procuring cause of our reconciliation and salvation as the atoning work accomplished by the Son of God upon Golgotha's cross. If, therefore, gentlemen, you will repent and believe, you will *have peace with God through our Lord Jesus Christ* and may, while living here, enjoy unhindered fellowship with God, the Father Almighty, and then dwell with Him forever amid the indescribable delights of the heavenlies.

"Young gentlemen, as I look into your faces knowing what are the temptations that surround you, and the problems of life, and the tremendous issues involved, I say, you need God on your side in order that life may be pure, noble, and heroic; that it may be a success; that it may be worth living, to say nothing of the hereafter. I, therefore, by the most sublime considerations man can possibly consider, exhort you to now open your minds, hearts, and lives to the truth as it is in our Lord Jesus Christ and get right with God."

Dr. Munhall always concluded this discourse by relating the story of his conversion and telling of some of his subsequent experiences.

CHAPTER TWELVE

THE WHITE LIFE

The Reverend W. E. Biederwolf is one of the most successful evangelists of the present day. If one feature of his work should be more emphasized than another, it is his ability to influence men. This chapter is an abridgement of his sermon on the "White Life." God has used it to turn the attention of thousands unto Himself in many cities and towns where it has been delivered. As a result of it, hundreds have accepted Jesus Christ as their Savior.

> "*How can a young man keep his way pure?*
> (Psalm 119:9)

"Scripture – 2 Samuel 18.

"David is king of Israel, and Absalom, his own boy, is arch-conspirator against the throne. David has fled from Jerusalem and gone to a city beyond the Jordan, while close at hand in the forest of Ephraim a hard-fought battle is in progress, and at the head of Israel's army is the king's own son. Great issues are involved; the throne of David and his life as well are at stake. The king is at the gate of the city while the watchman has mounted the wall to look for coming news of the battle. As he looks, he sees two men running alone; the watchman has no sooner told the king below than the men arrive in breathless haste with tidings from the field. The fortunes of the day have been with David's troops. The enemy has suffered defeat; the rebellion has been crushed; and its leader, with three arrows through his heart, is hanging by his hair among the boughs of an oak. But while the returning troops are shouting their songs of triumph, the king, brokenhearted, goes up to the chamber over the gate to weep, and as he goes thus, he says, *'O my son Absalom, my son, my son Absalom! Would I had died instead of you, O Absalom, my son, my son!'* (2 Samuel 18:33).

"David was weeping over a wasted life. What splendid opportunities this young man Absalom did have for a bright and honorable career! He had had all that any young man could have. Fortune had smiled upon him and laid at his feet all the wealth, culture, and knowledge of an oriental monarchy. What prospects for the years to come, but what a miserable failure he made of it all! And he's not the only young man of whom I know or you know who has had opportunities just as good as his, but whose sun has gone down at high noon and whose life has been wrecked just as sadly as this one of which we speak.

"Absalom's career might briefly be summed up by saying, 'He was a fast young man.' He was rich. It might have been better for him if he had been poor. If wealth is the gift of fortune, then the smile of fortune often makes a man *un*fortunate. You may not have to work for your living, but you do have to work for your character, and the man who has his living made for him has a pretty hard row to hoe if, out of the God-given material of his own self, he carves and chisels a character that shall stand the test both of time and of eternity. Money is all right if honestly acquired. Get all you can, but don't *can* all you get. Use it for God and your family and it will bring a blessing into your life.

Great wealth has kept more young men away from a pure life.

But remember that great wealth has kept more young men away from a pure life than ever has the lack of it.

"Great wealth led Absalom, as it does so many young men today, into a high life, and a high life led him, as it does so many young men today, into a fast life, and a fast life is invariably the well-established road to hell. Young men, let your ambition rise higher than to be a mere pet in society. Life is a battle, a real stern conflict, and a good many of us have already found it out. It's not going to be fought with Quaker guns and toy pistols, and there isn't any room for the featherbrained dude, the young man with more collar than culture.

> The young man who would
> Be a woman if he could;
> But since he can't, does all he can
> To show the world he's not a man.

"And the young man who finds his chief delight in the

wine room and the billiard room and the cheap theater will find himself dampened for the struggle and defeated in the contest.

"Now, if we had time, we might easily see that Absalom was guilty of all the sins peculiar to his time, and long years after this scene occurred his old white-haired and brokenhearted father took up his pen and wrote these words: *How can a young man keep his way pure?* Now David knew what he was writing about from bitter experience; and if there is one man in this audience or in all this city whose life can't be made a little whiter and a little cleaner and a little more Christlike by the grace of God, then he's not like the rest of us poor fellows. God help us, and God help him too, for I truly believe that no man's life is so unclean as he who with brazen face will boast that he needs no cleansing whatsoever. God give us honest hearts just now.

SABBATH DESECRATION

"What about Sabbath desecration? The former holy hush of God's best day has given way to the rabble-rush for pleasure and the greed for gold. If a man had given you six dollars, it would be pretty mean to steal his seventh and last one, wouldn't it? And it seems to me the same principle ought to keep a man from using God's seventh and sacred day in a way to please himself, when God has already given him six days in which to attend to the business and pleasures of this world. It may be there are some here who have already desecrated this day, and I want to ask you, If God lets you live to see the light of another Sabbath, will you spend its sacred hours so that at the going down of its sun you can say, I have lived this day just as I would have lived it had I known I was to meet my God at its close?

PROFANITY

"What about the sin of profanity – this high crime of taking the name of God in vain with almost every sentence that some men utter? I wonder if there's anybody here that needs to have his way cleansed from a thing like that. I sometimes feel a sense of pity for the victim of certain habits, but there's no sin that's so absolutely senseless and so little to be excused as this habitual scorching the lips with the name of the most Holy God in profanity. The man who does it without effort or desire to cease from it is low-grained in his fiber and altogether unworthy of being recognized as a gentleman. You're not having any trouble understanding me, are you? It's a sad commentary on men when a mother can't send her child down the street on an errand without his little heart being sowed full of the seeds of profanity before he gets back. I heard a father the other day utter a most damnable oath before his little seven-year-old boy. Man, you'd better be dead and in your grave than to be living with those given to you by God and be guilty of a thing like that.

DRUNKENNESS

"What about the sin of drunkenness, this awful vice

that holds in its clutch 250 thousand of the once fairest of our land, and sends seventy thousand of them every year down into a drunkard's grave? I read the other day that the beer that is drunk in this country every year would fill a canal forty feet wide and fourteen feet deep and twenty miles long. I know a lot of fellows who'd like to swim in a canal like that. It is told of Jonah in the Bible that he ran away from God and, entering a ship to go down to Tarshish, he paid the fare thereof. I don't know what he paid. He was a prophet, and maybe he traveled on half rates, but anyhow the distance was short, and it only cost him a trifle for his passage, but you know that he paid pretty dearly for that trip before he got through with it. And so many a young man has taken his first glass of intoxicating liquor and paid the price thereof, or had some other fellow pay it for him – only a few cents, five or maybe ten, but if he could have looked down the pathway of time for twenty years and seen the awful cost of that first glass, he would have shrunk from it as from a viper in his path.

GAMBLING

"What about gambling? I wonder if there is any need of a cleansing in this place from a thing like that. No doubt there is, and a great need of it too, unless this place differs from most others where I am privileged to speak in these days. Some of those engaging in it can ill afford to spare the few dollars that ought to go to cheer and brighten the homes and the hearts of the wives and little ones. I think a gambler is about the meanest, lowest, and most disreputable thing that passes for a man of anything that breathes under the sun. The man who, with a black heart under a white shirtfront, will take another man's money on the plea that he ran a chance of losing his own.

With every cent he wins and with every penny he loses, his hellish passion is fanned into a fiercer flame until he will sacrifice on the altar of his lust his money, his honor, his home, his love, and what were once his loved ones, and then will rattle his dice and shuffle his cards on the coffin of his victims and pocket the bloodred gold of his murdered kindred. Judas was a gambler, and he sold his Christ for thirty pieces of silver. I read in the Bible that they took the money and bought a graveyard with it, and called it in

I think a gambler is about the meanest, lowest, and most disreputable thing.

the Syriac language *Aceldema,* which means 'The Field of Blood.' And this afternoon, over every racecourse, over every faro table and gambling device, over every church fair or anywhere where a man or woman wins or loses what otherwise would not be theirs, simply because they have taken a risk and happened to hold the lucky number, I would write the words, 'Blood Money,' and brand everyone thus engaged as a dishonest man or a dishonest woman.

IMPURE IMAGINATION

"What about the sins of the imagination? Oh, these

imaginations of ours, how often they are unholy; this fairy land, the enchanted ground, the place of odorous flowers and rosy clouds and balmy breezes where, all unseen and undiscovered, this subtle power creates unholy scenes of lust, and dreams those ravishing, venturesome dreams. Entertaining the bewitching thought, it rolls it over and over in the mind like a sweet morsel under the tongue until the deed has been done and the sin committed a thousand times over in the heart, even though restraint may be practiced in the outer life. An impure imagination can pierce through anything to see a forbidden object; it can lend beauty to beastliness and transform a loathsome vice into a bewitching charm.

Once let an impure imagination be thus brought into play, it will set the whole of a man's sensual nature on fire with hell. There is not one fallen man or fallen woman – and notice I speak of a fallen man just as I do of a fallen woman; God only knows which one has fallen the lowest, but I utterly loathe this sentiment that would stone the woman and let the man go free, that would trod the victim of his lust down in the mire and let the man wipe his lips and step back into decent society – but I say you will not find one such man or woman whose fall did not come through a polluting preparatory process in which the imagination was indulged in the forbidden sweets of sin. 'Think well, and do well will follow thought.'

UNHOLY CONVERSATION

"What about these lips of ours and the sin of unholy conversation? In the presence of a depraved prostitute, you can hear words that would disgrace the foulest inhabitant of the lowest pit of hell, but how men of a fairly decent type can scorch their lips with the same stuff is enough to make a pure man sick in his heart. A private in the army said to me, 'Chaplain, what shall I do? The last thing I hear at night in our tent and the first thing in the morning is nothing but the foulest smut and indecency.' And my own ears were compelled to listen to literal battles of language to see who could put the filthiest things in the dirtiest guise. And the young Cuban lads that hung around the lines of the regiments, picking up a few words of *Americano* – that is supposed to stand for the best and most exalted that civilization can show – the very first words they were taught were those expressive of the dirtiest and foulest things that a rotten heart could imagine.

"Fathers, if you have a purehearted boy, you might better with thanksgiving see him go down to his grave than to see him forming associations with such fetid vultures of moral disease, and might better go there yourself than to live and be uttering such corruption in his presence. If I had a boy, I'd rather see him living in the slimy air of some foul dungeon with lizards and scorpions and venomous toads, if his heart were pure, than to have him dwell with men who deem a little smut and indecent stories things to laugh at, and then to see in the end a whole nest of hissing vipers wriggling in his heart. Foul language spreads poison worse than smallpox, and it can't be quarantined, but goes from lip to lip and heart to heart with its withering, damning curse. Like a slimy serpent it winds its venomous coils around holy manhood and pure womanhood and drags them through sensual mire down to hell. Where is the man who will take upon himself the vow of a white life? Let him begin with a white tongue.

Foul language spreads poison worse than smallpox.

UNHOLY ACTION

"And now one step further. What about the sins of unholy action? Do any of us need to have our way cleansed from that? Young men, boys, may I say a word to you as an elder brother? There is a sin that is blighting our young manhood in its early morning, and reliable physicians who are in a position to know, say it is well-nigh universal. Let me ask you to be warned and to shrink from it as you would from a viper in your path, for it will sting you to death.

KEEP THYSELF PURE

"And now but one thing more, and I refer to the human scoundrelism that looks upon a woman as the legitimate prey of a man's beastly passions and polluted appetites; the blackheartedness that sacrifices the pearl of a woman's purity to beastly lust; the foul seducer of virtue who, under the promise of speedy marriage, will take advantage of that which is best in a woman – her love – and then fling her aside and let her lie scorned and unhelped in her shame. When Paul wrote to Timothy, he said, *Keep thyself pure* (1 Timothy 5:22 KJV), and the doctrine that impurity is a necessity is a damnable fallacy. If there is a man in your city who calls himself a doctor and tells your young men that such a thing is a essential to their health, he isn't fit to go into a decent home in your town. And if there is such a one here now, who would dare to say a thing like that, let him stand up and say it now. Before God and man, you are a liar!

God would never have said, *'Thou shalt not,'* if it were necessary to do so, and all reason and best medical authority declare it to be a chief source of physical debility. He who is not pure is not a man, and out of respect to animals we must not call him a brute. I am not speaking of the man who is falling short, or about the man who is making an honest fight against the unholy passions of his life, but about the thing that passes for a man and has given himself up to that which is vile and unclean, and will even gloat over his work when it is done.

"Is there anything white about a man who will enter a home and, with all his gentility and smooth talking, win the esteem of the parents and the confidence of the daughter and blast it by his hellish, ravenous lust? Is there anything white about a brother who expects his sister to be purer than himself? Is there anything white about a man who expects his wife to be pure and is not pure himself? Sam Jones said it, and it is true: 'If there is any place in hell deeper and darker than another, it ought to be for that man who will go home at night from a house of shame and pillow his dirty old head by the side of his sweet, virtuous wife.' And I call upon you to enter into a crusade against the foul-mouthed man, to boycott the impure boaster and the betrayer of innocence until the blush of shame can never come to the face of your daughter or your sister, because society tolerates such men to move within its circle.

"Two things ought to be said just here: All these things increase just like the weeds in a garden, unless they are rooted out. Out in California where they drive the stagecoaches down the steep mountainsides, it is necessary to put the brake on hard lest the coach plunge down upon the haunches of the horses. There was some time ago a very godless driver who had been for forty years on a certain route. He was a vile, profane man, who often boasted that he feared neither God, man, nor the devil. At last, he was on his deathbed, and as he lay there his friends noticed him kicking out with his right foot as if he were reaching for something. They thought it must be too warm and they took off most of the covers, but still he continued to reach out with his right foot. They spoke to him but received no response.

At last his old chum, Joe, came and said, 'Bill, what's the matter? Isn't there something I can do for you?' And, looking up into Joe's face with a look that Joe said he never could forget, Bill said, 'My God, I'm speeding down the hill and I can't find the brake.' Speeding downhill and I can't find the brake! Young men, put on the brake at the top of the hill, stand today in the strength of God and your manhood, and you can live a life that an angel would be proud to own.

"The other thing is this: We're all guilty! You may not be a gambler, I may not be a profane man, and you may not be an impure man, but we all of us are sinners and have within us the root of sin from which these things spring. We are not perfect, and we need to have our lives cleansed. How shall it be done? Listen. *For as he thinks within himself, so he is* (Proverbs 23:7). *For out of the heart come evil thoughts* (Matthew 15:19). If the fountainhead of a stream is unclean, how can you expect clean water to flow down the river? And if the heart is unclean, how are you going to have pure thoughts to dwell in the mind, and pure words to fall from the lips, and pure actions to characterize the life? And now listen. *If we confess our sins, He is faithful and righteous to forgive us our sins* — thank God, it makes no difference about the past – *and to cleanse us from all unrighteousness* (1 John 1:9). You've tried to win the victory alone and you know how you've failed, but listen again: *For the law of the Spirit of life in Christ Jesus has set you free from the law of sin and of death* (Romans 8:2). Believe it and try it.

"And now I want you to listen to four or five brief reasons why every man of us ought to live the White life, the Christ life, which is the Christian life.

"The first is, *it is the manly life.* I have never heard of but one man who ever gave any real reason for not being a Christian, and he frankly confessed that he wasn't man enough. It takes a man to be a Christian; anybody can live the other kind of life. There are some men who are daring to refuse the surrender of their lives to God, thinking to do just as they please, as long as they please, and expecting God to save them when they get good and ready to let Him. Man, if you've ever thought a thing like that, never think it again, and lay claim to being a real man.

"Second, *it is the reasonable life.* I have heard of a man who said he was going to decide this thing in a reasonable way. He said that he would write down on one piece of paper all the reasons why he ought to be a Christian, and on another all the reasons why he ought not to be a Christian, and then he would weigh the matter in a rational way and decide like a reasonable man. And so, he began. He wrote first the reasons why he ought to be a Christian, and his pen just flew down the paper and up on the other side until it was all full of reasons. Then he began with the reasons why he ought not to be a Christian. He wrote down the number '1,' and there his pen stopped. He could not think of one single reason why he ought not to be a Christian. And you can't either. There are no such reasons.

Some men talk and act as though the Gospels were unworthy of the endorsement of a thinking brain, but friends, the brains of the world are marshaled on the side of the gospel. Mr. Gladstone was a brainy man, wasn't he? And he said, 'Forty years have I been in the service of my country, and I have come in contact with sixty of the masterminds of the kingdom, and they were all Christians but three or four.' Your martyred president was not too brainy to be a Christian. The current president is not too brainy to be a Christian. No, brother, come with all your intellect today and you will find yourself in agreeable company as far as brains go.

"In the third place, *it is the life of great blessing.* Every man who has tried it knows this is true. Why, man, you can lie down to sleep every night with heaven in your soul if you're living a Christian life. And oh, what it would mean for the home if father and husband were only a Christian.

"In the fourth place, *it is the heavenly life.* Paul says, *Those who practice such things will not inherit the kingdom of God* (Galatians 5:21).

"I have read the story of a man upon whom the drink habit had fastened its terrible grip; it took his wife and child from a beautiful home to a miserable garret. One day a message came to him while in a drunken stupor, saying to him that if he wanted to see his little boy alive, he must come at once. It sobered him instantly, and, going home, he found his boy with but an hour of life before him. He had been playing in the street and was run over by a large wagon and terribly crushed. As the father came and knelt at the cot, the little fellow took his hand and said, 'Father, I can't die till you promise me you will give up your sin and meet me and Mama in heaven.'

"'And,' said the man, 'with his hand in mine I promised God I'd make an honest effort to give up my sin, and promised my boy I'd meet him in the better world, and ever since that time I have felt the clutch of my little boy's hand pulling me higher and higher, and I know I can't help reaching heaven at last.' And, man, if you ever reach heaven, if in your redeemed state you ever meet again those you love, it will be when you take your stand for God with the other Christian men of this community, and by His help make an honest effort to forsake your sin.

"Let me now mention a last reason, and it seems to me it ought to stir all that is best and noblest in every man here. It is this: *Others need your help.* There are men here who could stand up today and say, 'I mean henceforth to be a Christian man,' and your whole family would come running into the kingdom of God. Because you have not had the courage or have not had the concern to take your stand boldly on the side of God, you have been standing in the way of those whom God has given you.

"I said this one time in Ohio, and a man well on in years came to me at the close of the meeting and said, 'Did you mean what you said?' And I replied, 'I did most certainly mean that very thing.' And as I took the big man's hand (for he was an unusually large fellow), his lips began to tremble and a tear appeared in his eye as he said, 'And to think of it that last year my nineteen-year-old boy was taken from me, and in all his life he had never heard his father pray.' And I said, 'Mr. Patton, give your heart to God tonight.' And he replied, 'By the help of God I mean to be a Christian.'

"The next night when the invitation was given, I saw him coming down the aisle with a young lady, and when he reached the front, he said, 'Mr. Biederwolf, this is my daughter.' The next night I saw that young lady sitting with another, and across the aisle was Mr. Patton with an elderly woman. While the opportunity was being given for people to come to Christ, I looked down among those who stood at the front, and there stood Mr. Patton with the other just mentioned, and calling me to him, he said, 'Mr. Biederwolf, this is my other daughter and this is my wife.' And there he was with his entire family inside the kingdom of God, because he had done at last what for many long years the Spirit of God had been constraining him to do.

"There are men here this afternoon who have been blighting the faith of your wives, and by your indifference to the things of God have been throwing wet blankets on the endeavor of the mother to train the little one in the way of Christ. There are fathers here today whose children not only have never heard you pray, but also in whose little hearts the tender sprout of faith and love is being frozen by your disposition toward Christ and the concerns of the soul.

"You have been dwarfing their souls and crushing out of their hearts every inclination to be pure and holy and Christlike. Father, in God's name, what are you doing? You've all doubtless heard the story; I tell it only because it is so forceful, the story of a man going out to his barn one wintry morning after a fresh fall of snow. He did not know his little six-year-old boy was following until he heard the little voice behind him, saying, 'Papa, I'se putting my feet in your tracks,' and looking back he saw the child stretching out his little legs and putting his feet in the place made by his father's in the snow. Fathers, that very thing is true of your child today. He is putting his feet in your tracks. Which way are those tracks leading?

"Mrs. J. K. Barney has been called 'the prison angel.' She has befriended more prisoners perhaps than any other woman of our day. Entering a New England prison one day, the warden said to her, 'Mrs. Barney, there is a young prisoner dying; we have sent for his mother, but there has been a wreck on the old Cape Colony Road, and she cannot arrive before her boy is dead. Won't you be a mother to him?' Mrs. Barney knew what that meant. She went up to his bed and talked to him about God and heard him say his faith was in Christ. Then he said, 'Mrs. Barney, they tell me Mother can't get here until after I am gone. Won't you say to her for me that I asked her to kiss me and say she would forgive me for all my sins against her?' And a few moments later, the young man was dead.

About an hour later the old train came rolling in. The mother's first inquiry was for her boy, and when told he was gone, she practically had to be carried up the stairs to where he lay. Mrs. Barney delivered the message, and what do you suppose the mother did? Just what your mother would have done if you had lain in the young man's place. She lifted back the sheet, and while tears streamed from her eyes, she kissed his pale face and said, 'Joe, your mother has come and she forgives you, but, O God, his father.'

"'Mrs. Barney,' the mother said, 'I suppose you think that this is a strange prayer to make, but when this boy was but nine years old, I heard him utter an awful oath, and when I reproved him for it, he said, "Why, Mama, I heard Papa say that last night." And when he was but twelve, I found him half-intoxicated. With these arms, I carried him into the house and held him until the stupor had worn away and heard him say that the one who gave him the drink was his father. Mrs. Barney,' she said, 'that was the beginning, this is the end,' and stooping down, she kissed him again and said, 'Joe, your mother has come, and she forgives you, but oh my God, the father.'

"Listen, men, while I tell you something better than that. A young lad of fourteen lay dying and the broken-hearted father was kneeling by the bedside. 'Willie,' he said, 'I have a sad message for you: the doctor tells me you are dying.' The little boy closed his eyes for just a minute and then, as a sweet smile stole across his face, he opened them and said, 'Papa, I'm not afraid to die, and when I die, I'll hurry up and find Jesus and tell Him I had the best papa in all the world because you taught me all my days to love Him.'

"Fathers, if your boy were taken from you tonight, could he say a thing like that about you? When the time comes that I must stand by the open grave of those I love, I want to be able to lift my face to heaven and say that while they were with me, I did all I could to help them be as God would have them be. Don't you? And God knows I could not say that, and you could not say it, unless we have been earnest and positive Christian men ourselves. And when the time comes when I must meet them again in the presence of the God of us all, I want them to be able to witness before Him that I was a help and not a hindrance to them on their way to heaven. Don't you? And if you do, will you say, 'From this day I mean as far as I can to live the life I believe God wants me to live'?"

CHAPTER THIRTEEN

A FATAL MISTAKE

Fred B. Smith has been called one of the greatest preachers to young men in modern times. I have no hesitation in saying that I have never seen another audience so moved as the audience in Topeka, Kansas, when Mr. Smith preached the following sermon.

All of his time is now devoted to this special work for men. He is himself so manly in his presentation of the gospel and so thoroughly imbued with the impression that every man needs Jesus Christ to complete and control his life, that his arguments and pleadings are well-nigh irresistible. He is a master in his control of audiences, and in his after-meeting work he is as strong as any evangelist I have ever known.

I saw more than three hundred men take a stand for Christ at the close of this sermon. Several thousand men were present, and the attention and interest manifested were intense.

He said, "I will read a few verses from the tenth

chapter of Mark's Gospel, beginning with the seventeenth verse.

> *As He was setting out on a journey, a man ran up to Him and knelt before Him, and asked Him, "Good Teacher, what shall I do to inherit eternal life?" And Jesus said to him, "Why do you call Me good? No one is good except God alone. You know the commandments, 'Do NOT MURDER, Do NOT COMMIT ADULTERY, Do NOT STEAL, Do NOT BEAR FALSE WITNESS, Do not defraud, HONOR YOUR FATHER AND MOTHER.'" And he said to Him, "Teacher, I have kept all these things from my youth up." Looking at him, Jesus felt a love for him and said to him, "One thing you lack: go and sell all you possess and give to the poor, and you will have treasure in heaven; and come, follow Me." But at these words he was saddened, and he went away grieving, for he was one who owned much property. And Jesus, looking around, said to His disciples, "How hard it will be for those who are wealthy to enter the kingdom of God!" The disciples were amazed at His words. But Jesus answered again and said to them, "Children, how hard it is to enter the kingdom of God! It is easier for a camel to go through the eye of a needle than for a rich man to enter the kingdom of God." They were even more*

astonished and said to Him, "Then who
can be saved?" Looking at them, Jesus said,
"With people it is impossible, but not with
God; for all things are possible with God."
(Mark 10:17-27)

"For many years in my life when I wanted to refer to some character that was beautiful and that would inspire high and noble living, I always referred to the 'Rich Young Ruler,' described in this Scripture. But suddenly the whole picture of his life and record changed from one of inspiration to one of warning, and since then, in increasing measure, this warning has intensified, and the seriousness of his error has become more apparent. I want, if possible, therefore to bring from this young man's experience a timely message of warning to other young men who may be following in the channel of his thought.

"There are four such warnings that I wish to speak of. The first one suggests itself to all of you. Always and everywhere, the preacher has never tired of referring to this young man *as a warning to the rich man.* From my boyhood, as I look back, it seems to me that that is the picture I have always had of this man. Over and over again, he has been held up as a warning to the man that was absorbed in getting wealth. Personally, I have no doubt about that warning being true. There can be no mistaking this message, and here is a clarion ringing voice warning every man on the question of money. I believe the words of Jesus Christ need but very little explanation. If ever there was a man that spoke plainly, that man was the Son of God. And when He said, *'How hard it is to enter the kingdom of God!'* I think He meant just what He said. If He didn't mean that, then I feel sure He would have said what He meant. Therefore, this message comes, first, with that warning in it.

"Two things I think are important, though. You will notice that when the disciples were so astonished at that statement, Jesus said, *'How hard it will be for those who are wealthy to enter the kingdom of God!'* I do not know of a place in the Bible where wealth as such is condemned, but everywhere running throughout it the right use of wealth is exalted. It is well for us to remember that this is not a sweeping charge against every man that is engaged in getting wealth. It is well for us to remember the other thing also, namely, it is not a question of the amount of money involved. One man may be as much kept away from God over getting ten dollars a week as another man is in getting ten thousand.

It is not a question of how much it is. It is simply a question of this: Has the struggle for bread, the conquest for gain, the battle of the commercial world, so consumed and so fascinated you that you have shut God out of your life? If it has, Jesus Christ speaks again about it when He says to you, 'With how much difficulty shall the man that is so consumed with things of this world ever enter the kingdom of God.' There is that warning, but I think it is only on the surface, and I feel sure that if that had been the only teaching that

Jesus intended to leave from this incident, He would not have given it a place in His Book.

"We pass to the second warning. Not only is that a warning to the rich man, but it is also a warning to another very large class of people. In the cycle of a year in my own life, I hear this more times than any other one objection to the religious life. When I press many a man about his personal obligation to live for God, he will answer me in this way: He says, 'It is true, I am not a religious man. I have never personally accepted Jesus Christ. I have never affiliated myself with organized Christianity, but I believe in it, and more than that, I am trying to live an honest, upright life.' Or, to be very quick with my words, that man says to me, 'I am not a professing Christian man; I have never entered the religious life, but I am living a moral life,' and he tells me that he pays his debts, that he is kind to his family, and that he tries to be a good citizen, and that therefore he feels his account is right with God.

"Hear me! There is not a man in all this vast audience, not one; there is not a man in the beautiful city of Topeka; there is not a man in the whole state of Kansas; there is not one man living in these United States, nor on this North American continent; there is not one man living today in the whole realm of the world that can stand up and say, 'My life has been equal to that of the rich young ruler.' Here was a moral man of the moral men. When Jesus asked him about that half of the commandments that had to do with his relation to men, recall what he said. Quickly this young man answered, *'I have kept all these things from my youth up.'* If there is a man in this audience that dare stand up and say that from his youth he has kept all of these commandments, I pause to let that man rise to declare that he has so lived. We know he has not, and I am sure that when Jesus held the interview with this young man, He was bringing out with His divine wisdom an eternal and forever answer to any man that would rob God of the glory of his life by saying, 'I am living a moral life.'

"There is many a man that seems to think there is some credit due him because he is out of jail. I suspect there are a lot of men in this audience who ought to be in jail, and if the truth was known about some of you, they would put you in jail before the sun goes down. The fact that you are out of jail does not prove very much. The religious life is not composed of negations; it is not a system of negatives.

> *There is many a man that seems to think there is some credit due him because he is out of jail.*

God not only wants you to keep from theft and from stealing and from adultery and gambling and from murder and the like, but – hear me, brother! – God also wants your *heart;* God wants your *life.* God wants your *service.* God wants your *ALL!* He will have that, or He will have nothing. No standard of morality, be it ever so high, is equivalent to the demand God has on every man's life through the grace of Jesus Christ. There is the warning to the rich man; and there is the warning to the man that is living only by human standards.

"There is another warning this young man brings. He teaches me that it is entirely possible for a man to be very, very near the kingdom of God, and then be forever lost. Look at this scene, if you will. This man was running out by the roadside, and as he ran, in his intensity he threw himself down on the ground upon his knees in salutation, and said, 'Oh Master, what shall I do that I may inherit eternal life?' Had it been the custom of the day, he could have reached out and taken the hand that was to be scarred for the sins of the world. This young man knelt there, and he heard the way of salvation, not from the lips of a faltering prophet, priest, or king. This young man heard the way of salvation from the very author of it, while He paused in His busy life to tell that young man what he must do to be saved. He had the privilege that some of us are longing for, and our souls are yearning for the hour when it shall burst upon us. This young man saw face-to-face the Savior of the world.

"This young man had the privilege. He looked into the very eyes and heard the words and stood in the presence of the Son of God, and yet we see him as he turns away sorrowing, and, so far as we know, he was a lost man.

"Only a little while ago, I rose on a Sunday morning early and read all of Luke's Gospel to see if I could find some character somewhere that would correspond with this young man that had at a later time come back in his life and repented and accepted Jesus Christ, but I could not find one. I do not know, but so far as the record is given us, after being so very near that line of decision, he drifted out into the world and went into a Christless eternity, without God, without hope.

"My warning is this: You are living in a land where there are more church spires pointing their majestic finger toward God than in any other land in the world, except one. More sweet chimes in America ring calling the people to God and to prayer than in any other land in all the world. More prayers are being said now than ever in the history of life. This is it: My brother, you note my message today! You may live in this land; you may live in a place where your streets are crowded with churches; you may hear over and over again the yearning appeal of the gospel. You may have been prayed over by the sweetest mother that ever sung a lullaby hymn to her child. You may have been counseled by the godliest father that ever lived. You may have been reared under the very dripping of the sanctuary of the church of God, and despite it all, you may be drifting out into the world and into sin, to go out of this life without Christ, without hope.

"Almost in the kingdom, and yet he was lost. Oh, I wonder how many men there are in this audience who can look back now to times when you were on the very verge of giving your heart to God and then somehow swung away from it. I suspect while I stand here now, that I am delivering the last message to some man. I suspect some man is standing on the mount this afternoon and is going to hear his last gospel message. Either accept it or turn away into the world to spurn God and trample it underfoot, and go out of life without God. The saddest hymn in all hymnology is that one we sometimes sing, 'Almost Persuaded.' You have been there – 'almost persuaded.' It closes thus:

'Almost' cannot avail;
'Almost' is but to fail!
Sad, sad, that bitter wail,
'Almost,' but lost!

"Let this man speak to you today from nineteen hundred years ago that it is possible for a man to be very nearly in the kingdom of God and then be forever lost.

"There is another warning. Not only does this incident warn me of the danger of becoming overconsumed in getting wealth, and of the danger of trusting alone in a moral standard, but also that it is possible for a man to be very nearly saved, and then be lost. I want you to get this last one. Get that scene before you vividly. The young man is running out by the roadside. He throws himself on the ground and looks up into the face of Jesus. He says, 'Master, what shall I do that I may inherit eternal life?' What did Jesus say to him? Did He say, 'You must quit that gambling, quit that stealing, quit that lying. Young man, put that impurity out of your life.' Not a word of it. Those things were foreign to his life. Hear it! Jesus looked on that young man and said He loved him, and then said, 'Young man, rich young man, honest young man, pure young man, noble young man, *one thing you lack!*'

"I know of no other four words in the Bible that carry such lifeless, mind-numbing power with them. *'One thing you lack.'* If I should ever write a book, these four words will be the theme of it. You may start today and you may go around the world, and as you go take a paintpot and brush and painter with you. As you travel around you may go to every penitentiary, where the young men pace back and forth behind the bars like caged lions with faces dulled. And when you come to the cell, you need not write over it the word *Murderer* or *Robber.* You may simply write over every cell in that penitentiary these four words: *One thing you lack.* And it will tell the secret of the life behind the bars.

You may go to two-thirds of all the insane hospitals, where the poor souls go with reason dethroned, and you may write over two-thirds of them just those four words: *One thing you lack.* Yonder where that poor mother kneels this afternoon and no rest comes to her body and no peace to her soul, there where she agonizes over some of you young men, you may simply write over her, as she bows there with a broken heart, praying for a prodigal son, *One thing you lack.*

"In every sad place, in every broken heart, in every place of sin, in all the cycle of the world, you may write over it these four words, and those words will tell you the secret of the ruin and sorrow and the broken heart.

"There are three things I want to say about that *one thing you lack.* First is this: Lacking that one thing, many a man has utterly gone to ruin in this world. In the Spanish war, sitting one day by the side of our tent in old Chickamauga Park, I noticed a young soldier climbing the mountainside towards us. I wondered what he could want. Despair was written on his face. Finally, he sat down on the hillside and bowed his head in his hands. I went down to him and stood by his side and said, 'Soldier, what is the trouble?'

"He said, 'I am a mean, miserable man, the most

miserable of all in this camp.' He was nothing but a beardless boy.

"I said, 'Tell me your trouble; I would like to help you.'

"He said, 'The day before yesterday, we got our first pay. Thirty-four dollars and sixteen cents I drew. When I left my home in Mississippi, my mother said she could not spare me, that I was her only support. I promised her I would send every cent I got back to her. I took that money and came down here to get a money order to send home. On the way I met some soldiers, and one of them had a whisky bottle, and I took a drink. I don't know where I have been, but I have been gambling and my money is all gone.'

"I said to that young soldier, 'What can I do for you?'

"He said, 'I thought I would come up and ask some of you if you would write a letter to my mother and tell her about it.'

"I said to him, 'What shall I write your mother?'

"He said, 'Write her that I was robbed. Write her that it was stolen from me. In God's name write her anything, but don't write her that I have been drunk and gambled it away.'

"As I stood by him, I said to myself, Is this young man a gambler? Is he a drunkard? Does he hate his mother? Is he deliberately wicked and cruel and mean in his heart? Just one trouble! When he left home that young man was lacking in one thing, and that was the power of Jesus Christ in his life. And lacking that had brought him to that place of sorrow and disgrace.

"Hear me, young men! Someday, if the raging torrent of sin sweeps over you and you lie on the rocks yonder, bruised, bleeding, and undone, remember what I said to you this afternoon. You will go there just because you lack this one thing.

"There is another thing I want to say about those four words. Mark it close! You may go and get everything in all the world that you ever dreamed of. Let your mind go out quickly over all the things you have ever thought you would like to do in the world. Sum it up now – of all the victories that you dreamed of winning, of the money you would make, of the fame you would have, of the wisdom that someday would be yours. Sum it all up, and I give you my word that if you go and get it all and leave out that *one thing,* your life is going to be a failure, and someday you will give that testimony before you leave this old world.

"I knew a man that from boyhood was often exhorted to live the Christian life, but always put off the day of decision. 'I am going to, but there is no hurry,' was many times his answer. After fifty years he was violently taken ill, almost the first time in his life. The doctor quickly told him it was a sickness unto death, that only two or three days at most were left for him, and that his *business* must be adjusted at once. He said, 'It is not *business* I want to adjust.' He sent for an old minister, and for forty-eight hours they tried in vain to bring him to trust in Christ. He refused to believe God would accept him, and the third morning, as the end approached, he talked with sons, daughters, sons-in-law, and friends, and to each he gave the same pleading: 'Do not make the mistake I have made.'

And with the old pastor hurrying a prayer to God

to save him at the last moment, with some friends trying through tears to sing, 'Jesus, Lover of My Soul,' he raised himself, and calling his oldest son, said, 'Hold my hand, boy, it is getting dark, I cannot see, it is a failure,' and he dropped back on his pillow, and his spirit winged its way to God. His dying words were: 'It is a failure.' In what? Money? No! He had accumulated a goodly sum. In the estimation of his friends? No! He was highly honored among men. In his home? No! He was one of the kindest of men. The failure was in this: that amid the busy activities of his life he had forgotten God, and when he lay down to die, he left as his parting message that sad confession: 'It is a failure.'

"My brother, go get gold until you can pile it mountain high. Go get wisdom until you can contend with Solomon. Go get glory until your brow can bear no more, but leave God out of your life, and someday you will go out of this world and say, 'It is all a failure.' I care not what else a man gets; if he leaves God out of his life there will be a blank there that with his own words he will wish he had not lived, and with his own words he will say that his life is a failure.

"The other side – what is it? I have just said that if a man got everything in all the world he would like to have, but left God out, his life would be a failure. Now get the other side of it.

"If you in this life meet defeat, if in this life at every milestone you have to pause and write, 'It has been a defeat for me,' if you will do what I say, your life is going to be a triumph. After all, there are only a few men who know what the largest blessings of this world are. Most men to whom I speak today are men who live a hard struggle; most men to whom I speak today are men who will go through a hard battle; most men to whom I speak today are men who will live in poverty and die in the struggle. This world showers its blessings in largest measure on only a few. Most of us will never be known outside of the county in which we live. Hear me, my brother, and mark it well. If you will give your heart to God and serve Jesus Christ while you are here, when you go out of this life it is going to be a victory! [Cries of 'Amen! Amen! Amen!'] It is going to be a victory as sure as I look into your faces.

"Pardon me if I use a personal illustration. Once a year I go out to my old farm home, there where the scenes are so familiar that they swing me back to the days of my childhood. And if there is a sadness about going there, it is this: somehow the sadness of the struggle of the life of my father and mother. My father is now a man whose hair is white – an old man, coming to the close of life. At times he has prospered, only in old age to have the uncertain wheels of commercial life swing against him, and he closes life soon with nothing of this world to call his own.

"A few years ago, when I went to visit them, I went with the express purpose of taking them away from that old farm. I felt as though the time had come for them to leave it. I stayed those days until the Sunday night before I was to leave the next morning. I waited until all were in bed and we were alone. We sat in that old dining room that is just as familiar, every crack and corner of it, as the faces of those I love best. Over on one side of the table sat my mother, with the old, leather-covered Bible in her lap. Every page of that old Bible is stained with tears of that dear old saint. On the other side sat my father. I said, 'Father and Mother, I have come out here now to ask you to leave the old farm and come away from it. It has been only a scene of hardship.' Mother said, 'No! I think we had better stay here. If any of the children or grandchildren are ever sick, here is a place you can come to.' I said, 'Mother, you must be so very lonely here now, and the old farm has just been a scene of hard work. You had better leave it.'

"Young men, when I am looking for the last time into the face of that dear old mother, I want to remember her as I saw her on that night. I am praying God to keep her memory fresh with me as I saw her then. She leaned across the table and pushed her glasses up on her forehead and said, 'We do get lonely here sometimes, but it is only for the children.' Then she said, as she held out the Bible and looked me in the face, 'Boy, we will never be so very lonely while we have this old Bible,' and she clasped it to her bosom and rocked to and fro.

"I went outside and stood alone, and as I stood there that night, I said, 'I can well go away and leave these dear old saints here in the keeping of God.'

"Catch my illustration? That is all the world they have. The money is all gone. They have never had any glory in this world. But I will tell you what they do have: They have a record of years of loyalty to the church of Jesus Christ. [Cries of 'Amen! Amen!'] And so far as I know, they are the richest people I ever knew in all the world. They are going out of life soon, and that is all they have. But when they go, I want you to know that that is going to be a place where we will stand around and we will shed some tears, surely; but we will stand around that grave, and if God gives me grace, I am going to shout, 'Hallelujah! This is victory!' [Cries of 'Amen! Bless the Lord!']

"Listen to me! Most of your life is going to be defeat. You might as well face it now. Most of the things you expect to do you will never accomplish. If you truly and loyally give your heart to God and serve Jesus Christ, a stranger though I am to you, I will give my word that someday you will go out of this life, shouting, 'Victory! Glory to God!'

"There is a question I want to ask, and then I am done. Up yonder in Dakota it was asked of me before I was a Christian. I was riding on a railway train with three men. As the train whirled along, we had two seats turned together, and our conversation was not that of Christian men. The train stopped at a little station, and as the passengers were going out, there came past me an old minister. I didn't know he was in the car, for if I had known he was there, my conduct would have been different – I never saw the day but that I respected the ministry. He leaned over and looked at me.

"I don't know who that old man was; I don't know his name; I don't know his home; but that strange old minister stopped at the car seat beside me and said, 'Young man, will you answer me a question?' I said, 'Certainly, sir,' and I blushed as I saw I was in his presence. He said, 'Young man, why don't you live like you want to die?' He didn't wait for an answer, but walked out of the car. We rode on in silence to the station where I was to get off. I went to the hotel and into my room, locked the door, and then back and forth I paced, as I said to myself, 'Yes, why don't I live like I want to die? Why don't I live like I want to die?' I never got that question out of my ears. I want to give it to you today.

"Young man, there is going to come a day in your life when you will pray! Yes, you will! I care not who you are, even if your heart be as hard as a rock. You may be able to listen to the gospel today and it never touches a tender place in your life. You may have rejected Jesus Christ until it has become a common thing to you. But hear me! Every man in this audience will pray someday! It may be too late, but you are going to pray! And the agony of your soul will go out in that last prayer you offer. I know you!

"You feel strong, don't you? You can stand up in the power of your physical strength and can curse and damn and swear and drink whisky and gamble. But you will pray! Yes, you will. You will pray, and someday we will find you on your face crying for mercy! You will cry, 'Oh God, be merciful to me, a sinner.' One of the meanest and wickedest men I ever knew was a man that lived in our village town. He was a gambler, a blaspheming man. But the day when he thought he was going to die, he ran out of the village and threw himself on the ground and cried so a hundred people could hear him!

"You will pray! Yes, you will. Some of you men, hear me! Before the snow flies over these prairies again, some of you will send a hurried message for one of these preachers to 'Come quick! I am dying.' You will call a preacher to your side to pray for you, and you will want him to stand over your grave and say a prayer there.

"Prince Henry, that dauntless young man of the early history of England, that young man that defied God and God's people, when he was twenty-seven years old, was told, 'Prince, you are dying.'

"He said, 'What? Dying?'

"'Yes,' they said, 'you are dying.'

"Do you remember his words? He said, 'Tie a rope around my body and drag me out to an ash heap and let me say my prayers!' They tied a rope around the body of Prince Henry, and as they started to the ash heap the cord was broken and the spirit of him went out to God before he got to the ash heap to say his prayer.

"I want to read four actual prayers. Listen, while I read you the prayer of Voltaire, that man that damned God and defied God's people; but hear him when he died! 'I am abandoned by God and man. I will give you [his physician] half of what I am worth if you will give me six months of life. Then I shall go to hell, and you will go with me. Oh Christ! Oh Christ Jesus!' That was the prayer of Voltaire as he went out.

"Listen while Thomas Paine, author of *The Age of Reason,* prays. 'I would give worlds, if I had them, that *The Age of Reason* had never been published. Oh Lord God, help me. Oh God, what have I done to suffer so much? Oh, there is no God. But if there should be one, what will become of me? Stay with me, for God's sake, for I cannot bear to be left alone. Even send a child to stay with me.' Oh yes, Thomas Paine prayed!

"Listen! Listen to another prayer by D. L. Moody. 'Earth is receding, heaven is opening. God is calling me. Let me go.' And Moody, the mighty man, *fell asleep* (Acts 7:60; 13:36).

"Let me give you another one. 'Good-bye all. Good-bye. It is God's way. Nearer, My God, to Thee.' And President McKinley went out to be with God.

"I am a stranger here. I have never been in this town before; I never expect to be again. I look into your faces only today and once only. My young man friend, I part with you. May I ask you this question: Why not be a man and live like you want to die?"

CHAPTER FOURTEEN

LIFE OR DEATH

Thin his sermon was preached by the Reverend Frederick E. Taylor, pastor of the Central Baptist Church of Brooklyn. It has pleased God to use it in a remarkable way, and to those who know Mr. Taylor, this is not at all strange, for very few men are more thoroughly consecrated and few that I have known have more of a passion for reaching men with the gospel than he has.

Mr. Taylor was in such great demand for the holding of evangelistic services in the interest of men, that at last on the advice of his brother ministers he resigned from his church. He is now devoting his time to the general evangelistic work, in every city preaching special sermons to men, with remarkable success. He begins his sermons thus:

"I call heaven and earth to witness against you today, that I have set before you life and death, the blessing and the curse. So choose

life in order that you may live, you and your
descendants. (Deuteronomy 30:19)

"The last words of our friends are always the most effective. The boy who has been disobedient to all authority of mother or father, listens attentively to the words of counsel, advice, or request as they fall from the lips of the dying parent, and resolves that now he will obey, no matter what the cost of obedience may be.

"These are the last words of one of the greatest men the world has ever known. Moses was a great man. He was great as a statesman and as a lawgiver. So great was he, indeed, that after four thousand years, we find the legal systems of the world based upon his words. He was not only great as a statesman and a lawgiver, but he was also a wonderful leader of men. Men like Alexander, Napoleon, and Grant have marshaled mighty armies, but Moses marshaled and controlled for forty years an army of men, women, and children numbering millions, and so completely was he master of the situation that in all those years there was never any need for a change of commanders.

"And now he is about to give up the command. He has received word from the Lord that he is to come home to heaven and receive his reward. As the evening shadows gather around his life, he rehearses before the people the story of God's dealings with them. He tells them the story of their deliverance from Egypt, and he sets before them their unbelief and their failure to respond to the will of Jehovah. He reminds them that whenever they have obeyed God, He has blessed them;

whenever they have disobeyed, He has punished them. 'Now,' he says, 'I am about to leave you, another is to take my place, and he will guide you into the promised land.' Then mentioning six blessings, he says, 'If you obey God, these will be yours, but if you disobey, these six curses shall come upon you, and he mentions these (Deuteronomy 28:3-6). And then, with great solemnity, he urges upon them the duty of choosing that which will bring the blessing of God. *I call heaven and earth to witness against you today, that I have set before you life and death, the blessing and the curse. So choose life in order that you may live, you and your descendants.'*

"It is a solemn moment in the life of any man when he stands facing the question of life and death. It is a solemn moment for men here today, because whatever else shall be the outcome of this meeting, I intend to set before you life and death, the blessing and the curse, so that if in the days to come we shall face each other at the judgment seat of Christ, I shall be able to say that on one occasion, at least, you came face-to-face with the claims of God upon your life. I want to be able in that day to say, in no unmistakable terms, that I set before you the reasons why you should choose life instead of death, the blessing instead of the curse.

It is a solemn moment in the life of any man when he stands facing the question of life and death.

And when I urge you to choose life, let me say that by choosing life I mean that you should choose Jesus Christ as your Savior and Lord. To choose life is to choose Christ, and to choose Christ is to find life. He is the way and the truth and the life, and until men know Him, they do not know the meaning of the word *life*. *'I came,'* said He, *'that they may have life, and have it abundantly'* (John 10:10). There are hundreds of reasons why a man should choose life, but out of them all I want to suggest just four, any one of which, as it seems to me, ought to be enough to lead a man to God.

I.

"*Every man ought to choose Christ because all men need Christ.*

"In every meeting like this there are men who, stirred by the influence of the service, go out firmly resolving to live a different life. They agree with the speaker, they believe the story of the gospel, and they have a desire for a better life. And certainly no one should find fault with a man who desires a better life. But suppose some man goes out today and, like many others, he decides that hereafter he will live a clean life. Suppose for the moment that this man lives to be fifty years older than he is today, and in all that time he never commits another sin. This is an impossible thing, of course, but for the moment let us suppose such a case. Now would that man be saved? Would he, because of these years of righteousness, be entitled to an entrance into the heavenly world? No! But you say, Why not? For fifty years of clean living is not a man entitled to heaven? And again I answer, No.

"In the first place, because no man will ever be saved

because of what he has done, but by that which Christ has done for him; and in the second place, he cannot be saved for the reason that he has not been cleansed from the sins already committed. The sins of all the years up to this time are still with him. Day after day and year after year he has been piling them up until they are mountainous, and nothing that he can do will ever atone for them. The sins of thought and deed, as well as the sin of rebellion to God's will, have never been purged from his life, and until the blood of Jesus Christ rolls over his soul, he will not be entitled to an entrance into the heavenly world.

If by an act of righteousness, if by any amount of pure living we can be saved, then Calvary is a farce, and Christ was crucified in vain. No, the Scriptures are right: *All have sinned and fall short of the glory of God* (Romans 3:23); *without shedding of blood there is no forgiveness* (Hebrews 9:22), and the young man should choose Christ so that he may be cleansed from sin. Not only does he need Christ to get rid of the sin already in his life, but also to keep him from the possibility of failure after he has been cleansed. Many a man is afraid to stand up and acknowledge Christ as his Savior because he fears that he will sin again within twenty-four hours and bring reproach upon his Lord. But Christ not only saves us but also keeps us, and those who put their trust in Him are kept by the power of God through faith unto salvation.

"But there is another reason why you need Jesus Christ, and that is because you can never fulfill the purpose for which you were created until you have Him in your life.

"No man is ever a man until he is a Christian man. When God made man, He made him foursquare. He gave him a physical side to his nature and an intellectual and social side to his nature; but He did not stop there, for He crowned the whole man with spiritual life, and this was meant to dominate the whole man. There are many three-sided men in the world today. They look alright in the eyes of men, but in the eyes of the Lord they are sadly deficient. A man may develop his body until he has the strength of Eugen Sandow, the bodybuilder; he may cultivate the social side of his life until he becomes a veritable Beau Brummell; he may educate his mind until he becomes a genius, but if he has only these, he is a failure, and he is of all men most miserable. Not until he has been touched by the Spirit of God and has flowing through his life the life of Christ does he become a complete man.

"Some years ago, in a little town in the West, a crowd of men were gathered around a store window. A large American eagle was in the window. Fastened to one of its feet was a chain, and this was secured to a ring in the floor of the window. The bird was absolutely indifferent to its condition. It was a splendid picture of fallen greatness. While the men were looking at the bird, a tall, young mountaineer elbowed his way through the crowd and, after looking for a moment, walked into the store and asked the proprietor how much he wanted for the bird. The man said two dollars. The young man took some money out of his pocket and paid for the bird, and the storekeeper unfastened the chain and handed the eagle to him. He carried the great bird down the street, followed by the crowd. Coming to a large billboard fence with a ladder against it, he climbed the ladder and placed the eagle upon the top of the fence.

Unfastening the chain, he came down. The bird remained motionless for a moment, then noting that he seemed to have more freedom than usual, he

God intended that men should live in fellowship with Him.

opened his eyes and glanced around. Then, as if to be sure of his power, he stretched out one great wing and then another, and then with a hoarse scream he soared up toward the sun, while the crowd sent up a cheer. 'I used to see that bird way up on the mountain where I tended sheep,' said the young man, 'and when I saw him chained down in that store window, I could not stand it. He belongs up above and was never meant to be in such a place.'

"And, friends, God intended that men should live in fellowship with Him, and when He saw us down here chained by sin, unable to realize the purpose for which we were created, He sent Jesus Christ to free us, and the cross of Calvary is the price of our freedom. And if we will but accept Him, we may live above the clouds of this world in fellowship with God.

"The second reason why you should choose Christ is:

II.

"Because it is a manly thing to do.

"I have said that a man is never a man until he is a Christian man, and I want to emphasize this. There was a day when, if a young man became a Christian, he was thought to be a milk-and-water sort of fellow who had none of the elements of manhood. But that day has gone forever. Men are beginning to realize that it takes all there is of a man to be a Christian. The manliest men this country has produced have been Christian men, and the man who thinks that a man loses any of his manliness by surrendering his life to Jesus Christ has a great deal to learn about real manhood. There came a time in the life of James A. Garfield when, at the top of Mount Holyoke, with some fellow students, they decided to camp there all night. When bedtime came, young Garfield took a New Testament out of his pocket and said, 'Fellows, I always read a chapter out of this book and offer prayer before I go to bed, and with your permission I will read aloud and offer prayer.'

Was he any the less of a man for that action? When Abraham Lincoln went to Henry Ward Beecher one night during the Civil War and spent the night on his knees with Mr. Beecher, asking God to save the country, did he lose any of his manhood? When William E. Gladstone sat down by the side of a sick street sweeper in one of the lowest shacks in London and read the Scriptures and prayed with him, was he any the less of a man? I do not need to press the question; every man here knows that these men were manly men and their relation to God only puts them upon a higher plane in our estimation. The fact of the matter is that the more manhood a man possesses, the more likely he is to be a Christian man. I have had many excuses offered me by young men for not becoming followers of Christ, but I have never had but one man give what I should call a reason.

"I was conducting a series of meetings in a well-known university some years ago, and when the last night of the meetings came, the hall was filled to overflowing. A number of the students had come out for Christ during the meetings, but there was still a number of them who were holding back. One of the men who attended the last meeting was a prominent football player, and was in fact one of the leading men in the college. At the close of the service, his chum, who sat beside him, stood up and publicly accepted Christ, together with a number of others. After the meeting was over, I met this football player and some others in a classroom. All of the men in the room came out for Christ except this one.

When I came to him, I saw that he was as white as marble. He was trembling from head to foot, and I knew that he was having a great struggle. Taking him by the hand I said to him, 'Will you take Jesus Christ as your Savior and follow Him?' He hesitated a moment, and then he said, 'I'm not man enough.' And he told the truth. It takes all there is of a man to be a Christian, and if some of those who are here this afternoon should tell the real truth, they would have to say, 'The only reason why I am not a Christian is because I am not man enough.'

"Another reason why every man should choose Christ is found in the fact that:

III.

"The service of Christ affords an opportunity for real heroism.

"We admire the courage of the man who, when the call comes for volunteers, leaves his home, and goes forth to face the bullets of the enemy of his country. And we should admire this courage. But let us not forget that moral courage is far superior to physical courage. Many a man who can face bullets without flinching will fall before a glass of beer. Men who will risk their lives for the sake of others sometimes have no courage at all in moral matters.

"Here is a young man and he has just left his home. He is sad-faced and heavyhearted. The doctor has just told him that unless the young wife whom he adores can have a change of climate and some of the luxuries that he has mentioned, she cannot get well. He loves her with all his soul and would be willing at any moment to lay down life itself for her sake. But here is a condition that he cannot help. His salary will not permit him to follow the doctor's orders. He enters the office and opens the safe and takes out the money for the day's business. He is all alone in the office. While he is counting the money there comes across his mind a suggestion that causes the hot blood to rush to his temples. Why not take some of this money? It will never be missed. You have nothing to risk, for you can put it back at your leisure.

And then all the forces of the hellish world begin

their awful work. On the one side is the wife whom he loves and the possibility of health and strength. On the other is the fact that years ago, he promised to follow Jesus Christ. The battle rages for a few moments, when, with a cry of agony, he flings himself upon his knees. 'O God, help me now!' And a moment after he stands up, the victory is won. That man is a hero!

Napoleon in all of his marvelous conquests never won a victory as great as that. Yes, men, the man who lives an out-and-out *I urge you to choose Christ.* life for Christ will have battles, and many of them, and this alone ought to appeal to young men, for what are we here for if not to fight battles? And what sort of a man is that who wants an easy time of it in this world? I long for men – real, dead-in-earnest men – men who will consecrate their lives to the service of Jesus Christ and then, to use the words of Mr. Speer: 'live with a vengeance and die with a snap.'

"And now, last of all, and perhaps most important of all, I urge you to choose Christ because:

IV.

"*In so doing you obtain eternal life.*

"*There is no other name under heaven that has been given among men by which we must be saved* (Acts 4:12). You ought to choose Christ because you need Him to cleanse you from past sin, to keep you from present and future sin, and to enable you to fulfill the object of your creation, because you are doing the manly thing when you do this, and you find an opportunity to develop a heroic character. But if none of these reasons move you, then let me urge you to choose Christ for the sake of your eternal destiny. You may not think you need Christ now, but the day will come when you will need Him more than you have ever needed anything in this world.

"While traveling upon the Long Island Sound Steamers, I used to notice that each boat carried two splendid-looking anchors. They were very nice to look at, but I could not see the reason for having them on board. We used to tie up at the wharf in Fall River, Massachusetts, and when we came to New York I noticed that they did the same thing here. And this led me to think that these anchors were carried merely for ornament.

"But one morning I was awakened by the blowing of whistles and ringing of bells, and I went on deck and found that we were in the midst of a dense fog. It was so thick that we could hardly see from one end of the vessel to the other. Just as I arrived on deck, I saw the sailors lowering one of the anchors. It went down into the water with a splash, the vessel swung around, and we were stopped. After awhile, the fog lifted and then I learned the value of an anchor, for right ahead of us was one of the other Sound Steamers. Had we gone on our way, we would have crashed into her with dreadful results. The anchor on that steamer saved our lives. And, my friends, when the fogs begin to gather and the things of this world fade from your view, the one thing that will prove valuable will be your hope in

Jesus Christ. And if you do not possess this, nothing but disaster and ruin await you.

"I am acquainted with a man who is an engineer on one of the railroads running out of New York City. Some years ago, this man, who is an earnest Christian, was addressing a meeting of men, a large number of whom were employees of the railroad. As he closed his address, he said, 'I cannot begin to tell you what Jesus Christ is to me. He has given me a hope that is very precious. Some years ago, every night as I neared the end of my route, I would look up to the top of a hill where stood a little cottage. And as we rushed down through the cut, I would pull open the whistle and let out a blast, and then an old lady would come to the door of the cottage and wave her hand at me. And as we shot into the tunnel, she would go into the house and say to her husband, "Thank God, Bennie is safely home tonight." That lady was my mother.

But the day came when we carried Mother out and laid her to rest. Then, night after night, when I pulled the whistle, an old man would come to the door and wave his hand at me, and I could almost hear him say, as he entered the house, "Thank God, Bennie is safely home tonight." But now,' said the engineer, 'they are both gone, and although I look up many times, I do not see either of the dear ones to welcome me home. But someday when I have pulled the whistle for the last time and the work of this world is over, I shall come to the pearly gates, and I am sure that as I draw near, I shall see an old lady waiting at the entrance with an old gentleman. And, as I enter, I shall see my dear old mother turn to Father and say, "Thank God, Father, Bennie is safely home at last."'

"Oh men, if for no other reason than for this, that it will mean the reunion of loved ones, the answer to the prayers of those whom we have loved long since and lost for awhile, I urge you to choose Christ.

"May God help you now to give free play to the noblest impulses of your life. Choose, choose now, and choose Christ.

> "*I call heaven and earth to witness against you today, that I have set before you life and death, the blessing and the curse. So choose life in order that you may live, you and your descendants.*"

J. Wilbur Chapman – A Brief Biography

J. Wilbur Chapman was an American evangelist, pastor, and author who was born on June 17th, 1859, in Richmond, Indiana. He grew up in a devout Christian family and attended local schools. Chapman became a born-again Christian at a young age and felt called to the ministry.

After completing his studies at Lake Forest College and Lane Theological Seminary, Chapman began his pastoral ministry in 1882 in Indiana. He served as a pastor in several churches before moving to Philadelphia in 1890, where he became the pastor of the well-known Bethany Presbyterian Church.

During his time at Bethany Presbyterian Church, Chapman's ministry gained widespread attention. He was a dynamic preacher who emphasized the importance of personal salvation and the need for Christians to live a holy life. He also believed in the power of prayer and often encouraged his congregation to pray for the salvation of others.

Chapman's evangelistic efforts were not limited to his own congregation. He traveled extensively, preaching at revival meetings and other events across the country. In 1895, he organized a series of evangelistic campaigns in Philadelphia, which drew large crowds and resulted in many conversions.

In 1903, Chapman resigned from his position at Bethany Presbyterian Church to devote himself full-time to evangelistic work. He joined forces with gospel singer Charles Alexander, and the two began a series of successful evangelistic campaigns across the United States and abroad.

Chapman's preaching style was characterized by his passionate delivery and his emphasis on the need for personal salvation. He often used anecdotes and illustrations to convey his message, and his sermons were known for their clarity and simplicity.

In addition to his preaching, Chapman was also an author. He wrote several books on the Christian life, including *And Peter, The Secret of a Happy Day*, and *The Life and Work of D. L. Moody*. He also edited several books, including *The Gospel According to Christ*, a collection of sermons by prominent pastors.

Chapman's family life was not without difficulty. In May 1882, he entered into the bonds of matrimony with Irene Steddom. Not long after, in April of 1886, their daughter, Bertha Irene Chapman, was born. Sadly, Irene Steddom Chapman passed away in the same month. After some time had passed, Chapman remarried on November 4, 1888, to a woman by the name of Agnes Pruyn Strain. Together they had four children, but tragically lost their son Robert during infancy. The surviving children were John Wilbur Jr., Alexander Hamilton, and Agnes Pruyn. However, on June 25, 1907, Agnes Pruyn Strain passed away. The, on August 30, 1910, he married Mabel Cornelia Moulton. This was his third and final marriage.

Chapman's evangelistic campaigns with Charles Alexander were highly successful, drawing large crowds and resulting in numerous conversions. Their partnership lasted for more than a decade, and they traveled to countries such as Scotland, England, and Australia, where they preached to large audiences.

In addition to his evangelistic work, Chapman was also a prominent leader in the Presbyterian Church. He served as the moderator of the General Assembly of the Presbyterian Church in the United States in 1912 and was a strong advocate for Christian education.

Sadly, Chapman's ministry was cut short when he died suddenly on December 25, 1918, while on a speaking tour in New York City. His death was a great loss to the Christian community, but his legacy lived on through his writing and preaching.

Chapman was a leading figure in the early 20th-century revivalist movement in America. He was known for his passion for the Gospel and his emphasis on the need for personal salvation. His dynamic preaching and evangelistic campaigns drew large crowds and resulted in numerous conversions.

Chapman's influence extended beyond his own ministry. He mentored several prominent pastors and evangelists, including Billy Sunday, who went on to become one of the most famous evangelists of the early 20th century.

Today, Chapman's legacy lives on through his writing and the numerous pastors and evangelists he influenced. His emphasis on the importance of personal salvation and the need for Christians to live a holy life continues to inspire Christians around the world.